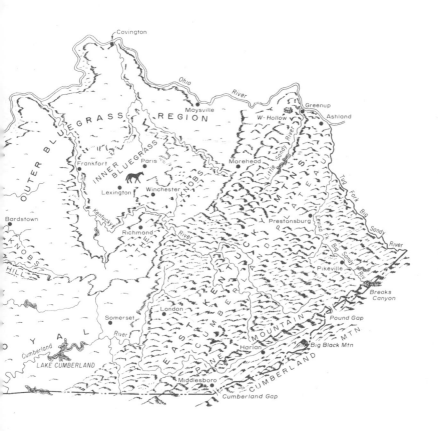

My World

JESSE STUART

THE UNIVERSITY PRESS OF KENTUCKY

Research for The Kentucky Bicentennial Bookshelf
is assisted by a grant from the
National Endowment for the Humanities.
Views expressed in the Bookshelf do not
necessarily represent those of the Endowment.

ISBN: 0-8131-0211-1

Library of Congress Catalog Card Number: 75-3552

A statewide cooperative scholarly publishing agency
serving Berea College, Centre College of Kentucky,
Eastern Kentucky University, Georgetown College,
Kentucky Historical Society, Kentucky State University,
Morehead State University, Murray State University,
Northern Kentucky State College, Transylvania University,
University of Kentucky, University of Louisville, and
Western Kentucky University.

Editorial and Sales Offices: Lexington, Kentucky 40506

*This book is dedicated
to Murray State University &
the people of the city of Murray*

Contents

MY W-HOLLOW

A TALK I MADE once at a small midwestern college was followed by a question and answer period. I'll never forget the first question. A young woman stood up. "Mr. Stuart," she said, "if you had only one choice, what would you say was the greatest thing that ever happened to you?"

I had never been asked that before, but my reply came in a split second: "The fact that I was born."

After some applause from my audience, I talked on. "Now, may I add something more. I would choose, if I had the choice, the same parents, the same little one-room cabin on a Kentucky hill. I thought, as a boy growing up, that it was the prettiest land in the world. Now after traveling in forty-eight of the United States and ninety countries of the world on six continents, I *know* it is the prettiest country in the world. So, I was a most fortunate youth."

The students kept an attentive silence.

"Of course, other states in America are beautiful, too," I said. "I have never traveled in any country in the world that has the varied scenery of the United States. In your midwestern states, here in the breadbasket of America, the most beautiful time of year is August, when vast fields of dark green corn grow out of the black glacial soil, and the corn is silking and tasseling. The second best time is when the wheat ripens and the fields are golden as far as the eye can see."

If these midwestern youths could have seen the place where I was born, with infertile soil on the steep slopes, poor to grow corn, vegetables, or anything but oak, pine, and sawbriars, they might not have understood why I was fortunate to be born there. But if they could have lived there through springtime, summer, autumn, and winter, each season bringing something new and mentally invigorating, I believe they would have agreed with me, as many have from other states who have visited Kentucky in all the seasons.

When Naomi and I travel across the United States or around the world and then come home again, I realize once more why I am fortunate to call Kentucky my land. Wherever we've been, whether the trip has been for three weeks or a year, we are always glad to get back. Whether our port of entry is New York or Honolulu, the state of states we hurry to return to is our Kentucky. And the county in Kentucky we hurry home to is Greenup County. It is just one of Kentucky's 120 counties, but this one is our county. Then the one spot in Greenup County we can't wait to see is W-Hollow and home.

Some do not feel the urge to travel, to discover their wider country. I wrote of my father once that he didn't have to go away from this place to find beauty, for he found it everywhere around him. He had eyes to find it. He had a mind to know it. He had a heart to appreciate it.

Each time I come back I rediscover my home. The hills and valley of W-Hollow are mostly our land by deed. It is also the land we own in our hearts. We feel this is true of all the people who have ever lived in W-Hollow. Whether or not they held deed to an acre of this land, they loved and owned it in their hearts.

My world begins, then, here in W-Hollow, the little core of my Kentucky, of my big United States of America, and then of the six continents of my bigger world.

This place is my flesh, bone, and blood. Here I know the clumps of ferns, the trees, the cliffs. Here I have put my hands on the bark of trees and looked up their tall bodies to the skies. I've done this at all times of year when I am out to see the new dress each season wears. I go out now, as I have always done, to see wild wings slice the air, to hear birds speaking in their many languages. I go out to hear the slithering sound over old leaves where the blacksnake crawls. I go out in the land of the fox, the raccoon, the possum, the bobcat, the woodchuck, the squirrel, and the deer. This is their W-Hollow, too. My land is their land. If food is scarce they don't go hungry. I feed them, and they know where to come. Here there is a reverence for life. A reverence for life must reach to all the world.

A long time ago I said that to come to W-Hollow you can take any road you please. You can come the way a crow flies or the way the wind blows. You can follow your nose. But the road that led in then was a wagon road, the first three miles of it. The rest was a cow path, a goat path, a rabbit path, a fox path, a mule path; whatever you wanted to call it. The road was the color of sand rock, a pied copperhead turned on its back in the sun.

My people found their way here along many roads. The majority of my mother's and my father's people sleep in the country church cemeteries here in East Kentucky. It is truly their land, as well as my land. Their names were Stuart, Meade, Hilton, Pennington, Chandler, Greene, Preston. They moved up from Virginia through Pound Gap into the Big Sandy Valley. Then, when the clan wars came, my grandfather moved down to Greenup County. Much later he went back to Lawrence County, to his beloved Big Sandy River, but he had too many enemies there and was murdered. He loved his land, as I do mine.

3

He said the water in the Big Sandy River was his blood; his flesh was the Lawrence County earth that nurtured him, and the Lawrence County stones were his bones. I didn't understand that when I was a child, but I've never forgotten his words.

My father, Mitchell Stuart, known as "Mick," married Martha Hilton in Greenup County. They lived together forty-nine years before my mother's death. My father's death was three years later. In those forty-nine years they lived in six different houses, all within a one-mile radius. My father's plow and my mother's hoe turned over all the pebbles and stones and much of the ground on hill and bottom in this valley. They planted millions of steps here.

My mother had seven children. Two of my brothers died young, but two boys and three girls still live. We grew up on the foods we grew from this soil, most of which is considered poor land. My mother and father rented land and share-cropped until I was twelve, when my father bought fifty acres of land. That was all he ever owned. But he told me I should buy land while I was a young man and hold onto it. Land didn't grow, he said, but populations did and we had to save our land for the generations to come.

So piece by piece, over a period of twenty-eight years, I have bought all the land my parents ever rented. Now I have approximately a thousand acres. This land will never be destroyed, nor will its timber and wildlife, as long as I live. My sisters, nephews, nieces, and I now own nearly all of W-Hollow. We have one of the most beautiful little valleys in Greenup County, in the eastern mountains of Kentucky, in all of Kentucky, in the United States, in any country of the world. This is saying a lot, I know. But I have visited many times in Scotland, England, Wales, Ireland, Germany, France, Switzerland. I have seen the small valleys in these countries. But they are not like W-Hollow.

I grew to manhood here, eating food grown from this soil. We never bought anything from the stores but salt, pepper, soda, baking powder, and sometimes sugar, for we often sweetened with sorghum and wild honey in the early days. Our mother nursed her children; never was one of us on a bottle. In the early days we had wild game, then later our own pork, beef, and mutton. On this food I grew into a broad-shouldered block of a man, just over six feet, weighing 225 pounds. My brother James grew to six-feet-five, a broad-shouldered 200 pounder. Our three sisters grew to be husky women, mentally and physically energetic.

As I grew up here I read the landscapes, the streams, the air, and the skies. Later on I would remember and write about those fortunate years and my earth reading. I took my time. I had plenty of time to live and think as I grew up in a world that I came to love more and more. I didn't know then how good a world it was to grow up in. It became the inner core of my expanding world. I told the students at that midwestern college the truth when I said that the most important thing in my life was being born, and born in W-Hollow, Kentucky, on a hillside in a one-room shack.

My education began in W-Hollow. Before I was six I made forays into the woods alone, climbing trees and looking into birds' nests. I remember once climbing up a tall, slick-barked chestnut tree and looking into a crow's nest that had three light blue eggs as large as the hens' eggs I gathered each afternoon. I didn't destroy those crow's eggs. I left them alone, for the old crow was flying over the tree and making a fuss. I slid down the tree faster than I'd gone up.

I knew the snakes, those that laid eggs and those that gave birth to their young. I learned the names of wild flowers, trees, berry vines. I memorized a forest's flora and fauna. I studied without an instructor. I was self-taught, building a foundation from which to plunge into

5

the life ahead of me, beyond W-Hollow. When I lost my brother Herbert I was without a playmate. Not another boy my age lived nearby. I tried to make friends with wild animals and birds when I went alone and deeper into the W-Hollow woods and valleys and along the streams. I discovered about everything there was to discover. This was a fine place for a boy to grow from childhood to manhood.

I may have studied W-Hollow without an instructor but I did have an example. Later, when I wrote about the man who was my instructor through example, I called him "God's Oddling." He was my father. He came to this valley when he was sixteen years old and he grew up here. He was a young man before he went outside Greenup County. He was almost sixty years old before he went a hundred miles from home. For almost three-fourths of a century, he greeted his animals morning, noon, and night, fed them, bedded their stalls, and was kind to them. He planted potatoes on high hilltops in new ground to grow them good and big if the season had plenty of rain. And, as insurance, he planted some in the old land down in the bottoms, where, if the season was dry, there would still be potatoes. He raised tomatoes in new ground so they would be soft and flavorful. He was kind to the earth and it returned the favor. There has never been a better gardener in W-Hollow. He studied land, plants, and seasons each year. He never could learn enough.

It took so much work to make a living on this land that was considered nonproductive. There were human mouths to feed, swine to be fattened for pork, cows and other livestock to be cared for. And with all this my father had to pay half of his crops to the landowners. It took a lot of work. My father used to say, "It takes all hands and the cook to make a living here." When we had a bad crop season, he would say, "My nose is to the grindstone!" I learned later in life that a Stuart nose wouldn't remain long on a grindstone. It was already sharp and didn't have to be sharpened much more.

I was introduced to the hoe when I was six years old and to the plow when I was ten. I was strong for a young boy and I could do the work. So could my younger brother James in years to follow. Work with a hoe, cutting weeds and raking fresh clean dirt that had a pleasant smell, was for me an education. Watching plants grow, calling corn a beautiful flower when one of the stalks silked and tasseled, was also part of my education. Later I wrote a poem about corn as a flower.

One day in W-Hollow, when I was between nine and twelve, I was hoeing corn with my mother. My father was four or five rows above us on the hill plowing. He stopped his mule and plow, looked down the hill, and said to us, "On this cool morning we're really moving with our work."

Before my mother had time to speak I looked up at him and said, "Dad and Mom, someday I'm going to own all the land you've ever rented in W-Hollow!"

I didn't know what made me say it. This was one of my dreams that slipped out in words before I'd given it much thought. My father and mother laughed at me, but they never forgot my dream. In those years my father and mother lived in the house where Naomi and I live today. They rented it then. We own it now. My mother died in 1951 and didn't live to see me buy the last piece of land we ever rented in W-Hollow. My father, who died in 1954, did live to see it. He remembered my dream in the cornfield, and when I bought the last farm we had rented, he cried. He knew that I had paid twice the worth for some of this land. But with loving hearts and Stuart hands this eroded land is now improved to a worth thirty times what I paid for it. People from many places—even visitors from Kentucky's naturally fertile Bluegrass land—exclaim at its beauty. When I first bought it, it was largely covered with scrubby pines, sawbriars, broomsedge, and eroded ditches.

My learning in W-Hollow didn't end when I entered school. I found life and beauty along the two miles I walked each morning and afternoon. The path led to the one-room Plum Grove School, where I spent twenty-two months learning from books. Words on paper: it was a whole new world for me. I devoured and digested books as hungrily as I did the cornbread that we made from the corn we raised and had ground into fresh, flavorsome meal. I began to catch hints that the rest of the world was not like my W-Hollow.

At Plum Grove School I wrote my first compositions. I wrote about things I knew. Instead of buying ink I made pokeberry ink and I wrote a child's essay on how to make this ink. I said that ink made from pokeberries was better than that made from inkballs. I said that inkballs on oak trees were scarce. All the other students laughed. They bought commercial ink at the stores. My little essay about pokeberry ink made them laugh.

A little later, less than five miles away, I found another world at Greenup High School. With my elementary foundation of only twenty-two months at Plum Grove, the studies in Latin, algebra, and plane geometry, were no "breeze." But I met them head-on, the way I tackled in football. My early training in W-Hollow helped. So did my observation and training in nature and my familiarity with hard work. When I started to play football I found I didn't have to "get in shape" the way some of the boys did. I had become a physical force. Before my four years ended I was also becoming a mental force.

In high school we had to write and read aloud a theme a week. I had a wonderful English teacher, Mrs. R. E. Hatton, trained in the University of Missouri College of Journalism. She told us to write our themes on subjects we knew the most about. She became one of my favorite teachers of a lifetime. I think I was one of her favorite pupils. I wrote more than a theme a week for her. She would read, laugh, and mark down A's for me.

Two of the themes I wrote for Mrs. Hatton have been published. "Nest Egg" was published in the *Atlantic Monthly* and has been reprinted in college and high school textbooks around the world. I wrote it when I was sixteen years old. I used it later; so did others, in two colleges and a university where it brought twenty-eight A's. Good old "Nest Egg!" Where did I get it? In W-Hollow, from our chickens, before I was nine years old.

I finished Greenup High School without any particular honors. If my classmates remember me for anything, it will be for the themes I read aloud and for some hard tackles I made playing right guard during four years on the football team. I can't say I was the best player on that team. I couldn't surpass Paul Campbell, another farm boy, who outweighed me and was a bull. My consolation was that he didn't write themes or stories or poems, as I did.

When I graduated from Greenup High School, I was like a young hawk leaving its nest on wings strong enough to fly, a young squirrel leaving its nest in the hole of a tree, any of the young that I had observed leaving their homes to discover the world around them. I was ready to leave the ten square miles which included W-Hollow, Greenup, and the hill between, where I had sat on rocks and stumps to write stories and poems on my way to and from high school. They also included the Plum Grove hills over as far as the Little Sandy River. This was the area where I had grown strong to face a life beyond my hills, beyond W-Hollow.

My first venture was to Ashland, Kentucky, where the American Rolling Mills, now Armco Steel, put me to work. From standby labor I worked up to blacksmith's helper and then to blacksmith. I became such an expert with a sledge hammer that at a street carnival once I rang the bell forty-five times straight while people looked on and paid my fees. Each time I got a cigar for ringing the bell. I didn't smoke then. I gave the cigars away. But I knew how to hit to ring that bell.

I could have stayed on indefinitely. But the steel mills were not my dream, not even with the higher pay I earned as a blacksmith. The street carnival wasn't my dream either. I got fired after two weeks, for giving free rides. In my youth I had dreamed of going to West Point. My father's people, Stuarts, had been fine soldiers and loved the military. But I couldn't get an appointment to West Point. It was a matter of politics. Democrats were in power and although I had a Democratic school teacher working for me, my people were all Republicans and I was denied. Later, while doing military service at Fort Knox, Kentucky, in the CMTC (Citizens Military Training Corps), I was glad that I had not gone to West Point.

But there was still my dream of more education. I had little money and time was going by quickly. Where would I go? I had had my dreams, big ones, of where I would go to college: Harvard; or the University of Virginia in the land of my father's and mother's people; or the University of Edinburgh, Scotland, in the land of the Stuarts; or the University of Missouri School of Journalism, where Mrs. Hatton, my Greenup High School teacher, had been educated.

From my boarding house in Ashland, Kentucky, near the steel mills, I wrote to all of these schools. But the expenses were prohibitive. My father was working now on a railroad section as a laborer, making $2.88 for ten hours' work. He was still in debt with his "nose to the grindstone." I would have to go it alone.

I packed and left the steel mills and the wage security they had given me. I had paid all my debts, for I hated debts. I was as free as the blowing wind. I hitchhiked to find a college, any college that would take me. If I couldn't go to the big ones, I would take a small one, any college that would accept me. My mother had said to me once, "I want you to grow up and be such a man that when you walk down the street in Greenup, someone will look at you and say, 'There goes Martha Hilton's son.'" I never forgot her words.

In my search for a college I was turned down twice, but at one of the schools I was told to try Lincoln Memorial University at Harrogate, Tennessee. I had never heard of this school but as soon as I had its name I was off and moving toward it. And sure enough, I was accepted, with only $29.30 in my pocket. I wasn't worried. I knew that if I could get work I could make it. I had a strong W-Hollow body, W-Hollow and steel mill muscles, and an alert and curious mind because I had walked as a lonely boy over W-Hollow with my head full of dreams. I had had time and space in which to grow up.

In my three years and two summers at Lincoln Memorial University I achieved enough to make my teachers, fellow students, and the president, too, take notice. My first poem was published in the college paper after I got myself elected its editor. In three years my average was 2.2 out of a possible 3. I worked half of each day, dried pots and pans after meals, and had classes the other half. I set one record of never missing a meal in 365 days while I dried the pots and pans at LMU.

I was on the track team, running cross-country. I made a record here, too—in three years I never got a first place. I always came in second to a classmate, whose rural Georgia world had given him more size and stamina than my W-Hollow world had given me.

I never had a scholarship. My mother sent me two dollars. For the rest of my expenses I had to work in the dining room, on a farm, with a dairy herd, laying bricks for buildings, laying water lines, and cleaning out sewer lines. I worked with as much imagination down in the manholes, starting sewage flowing again, as I worked when I was hoeing the last row of corn on a long slope of a W-Hollow hill, finishing it before dark.

Destiny had pointed the road for me. Lincoln Memorial was the right place. Here I met a great, wild creative writing teacher. I worked hard for him. I wrote three books that were later published, and forty-three stories that later appeared in *Atlantic Monthly, Harper's, American Mercury, Esquire,* and other magazines. I had found myself. I was expanding more and more from the deep roots of my W-Hollow foundation.

11

Then destiny pointed my way to Peabody College in Nashville, where I was fortunate enough to have Dr. Alfred Leland Crabb as my teacher for three summers. Again, I worked at what I could find.

My final experience in higher education was a year of graduate work at Vanderbilt University. The minimum cost for a year at the university then was $1,500, but I had only $130. I lived on eleven meals a week the first semester. Then a fire destroyed the dormitory where I lived and with it the cafeteria where I worked. The fire took all my clothes but those I had on my body, my typewriter, my thesis, over five hundred poems, my stories, articles, essays, and notebooks. A trunk half full of written material was destroyed.

During the second semester I lived on a meal a day. This was not a new experience for me. I had known before what it was to be hungry. But it was a test of my physical and mental strength. I made better grades during my second semester at Vanderbilt than during my first.

At Vanderbilt, I worked under a great teacher, Donald Davidson. An excellent poet, a man who had ideas and dreams, who changed my life. He knew about W-Hollow and my mountains of East Kentucky, and he told me I had a great heritage. He said that I should go back to my country and write of it as the Scots had written of Scotland and the Irish had written of Ireland. I left Vanderbilt without a degree, but a term paper I wrote there "Beyond Dark Hills," became my fourth published book.

Donald Davidson's advice was good and I followed it. I wrote about the world I knew, and my writings spoke to people around the world. Later my foundation as writer, farmer, and teacher sent me to distant countries. My first such experience was at American University in Cairo, Egypt. I was invited to teach there because of my book *The Thread That Runs So True*, which tells of my teaching experience in Greenup County and just across the

Ohio River in Portsmouth, Ohio. And I will tell you how I got there.

After my difficult year at Vanderbilt University, I borrowed two dollars and hitchhiked home with a small handbag in my hand. I told my parents I was through with all colleges and universities—that I would never teach again.

I had taught successfully before I went to Vanderbilt. I'd taught a one-room rural school and I had taught a rural high school of fourteen pupils in a building where horses had been stabled. I was so successful with these fourteen, eight of whom later finished college, that upon the resignation of Greenup High School's principal I was employed to replace him. This was a successful year, too, scholastically and in athletics. Our school was really moving until I was told to ask for a raise in salary. I was getting $1,000 and I asked for $200 more, to make a hundred dollars a month. I was fired. Then I went to Vanderbilt.

When I returned from Vanderbilt in 1932, there was a crisis in the Greenup County schools. And at this time I was farming my father's farm, staying with my parents, where there was no scarcity of good food grown from the land, and milk, eggs, butter, and cheese from our poultry and cows. We had pork, beef, mutton, and spring lamb from the farm. In addition to farming I was writing poems as never before. Two years later they were published in a book titled *Man with a Bull-Tongue Plow.*

One quiet Sunday afternoon, three Greenup County school board members approached us at my home. They told me if I could qualify for a superintendent's certificate they would employ me as superintendent of Greenup County schools. I had enough education and teaching experience and I got my certificate. I was barely twenty-five, youngest county school superintendent ever to serve in Kentucky.

As an inexperienced superintendent, I was beset with

13

problems from the beginning. I couldn't believe our school system had fallen to such low standards. With the persuasion of my school board members I made more reforms than enemies. But the Great Depression was in full force and banks were closing all over America. Our bank closed with all our funds. But by speeches, persuasion, and the help of excellent teachers, we kept the schools going without money. Even so, I made so many enemies, my friends on the school board said it was best for me to leave after one year, for there was a danger I might be killed. I didn't receive my superintendent's pay until three years later.

In the meantime I sold hens' eggs for seven cents a dozen for postage stamps. A dozen bought three two-cent stamps and a penny postcard. On Donald Davidson's advice I sent poems to three large national magazines. My poems were accepted and I received real money. I won on Broker's Tip in a Kentucky Derby. I put all these dollars together. When I departed the superintendent's office, where my enemies were getting stronger, a friend of mine became superintendent and I was selected to become principal of McKell High School in the autumn of 1933.

I spent the summer in Nashville, Tennessee, where I lived at the YMCA. I paid two dollars a day for my room and I lived on two meals a day to conserve my dollars. Here I wrote *Cradle of the Copperheads*. On its 945 pages I poured out my anger. It is as powerful a book as I've ever written but it remains unpublished.

The four years from 1933 to 1937 were wonderful years. I tried to make McKell High School the finest high school in Kentucky. When I went out to lecture now, after *Man with a Bull-Tongue Plow* was published in 1934, I checked over other schools throughout the United States, and I brought back ideas for my school. *Head O' W-Hollow*, a collection of stories I'd written at Lincoln Memorial University, was published in 1936. I applied for a Guggenheim Fellowship upon Dr. Crabb's recommendation, and I received it. As soon as my fourth year ended at McKell High School, I took a leave of absence and went to Scotland, land of my father's people.

In Scotland I prepared *Beyond Dark Hills* for publication in 1938. But I also wanted to visit each shire in Scotland. I learned later that I had missed a small one in southern Scotland. I wanted to visit each shire in England, too, and I did. I wanted to visit each country in Europe to see where the people had come from who settled America, but I missed Andora and Romania. Romania wanted $12 for a visa; being of Scottish descent, I wouldn't pay it to see their country. I had $2,000 for this scholarship. I sold some stories for small fees to English magazines and some few to *Esquire* and *Collier's* back in America. When I returned to New York City, after visiting twenty-eight countries in Europe, I had $7.00. But I sold a story in New York before I got out of town. I always carried stories as well as cash.

When I arrived home in 1938, there was a new principal at McKell High School. My "absence on leave" didn't mean security of position. But I was employed at Portsmouth High School, Portsmouth, Ohio, where I taught the first remedial English, according to record, ever taught in America. I didn't use a textbook. I used a newspaper, the *Portsmouth Times*. And this worked, too.

I left Portsmouth High School in 1939 to farm, to raise sheep, and to write. I returned to my old home to live with my parents.

One morning after my father had gone to his work as a laborer on the Chesapeake and Ohio Railway tracks, Mom and I had just finished milking our eighteen cows by hand. In those days we separated the cream from the milk and sold it. As we were walking to the house, Mom surprised me when she said, "Jesse, your father and I have been talking. You've been a wonderful son to us and you're still with us and you'll be 32 years old in August. We think you ought to get married!"

I laughed loudly, "Have you got a girl picked out for me?"

"Yes, we have. She's Emmett Norris's daughter, Naomi Deane."

"Well, I believe you've selected the right one," I said. "But would she marry me?"

On October 14, 1939, I married my childhood sweetheart, Naomi Deane Norris. We settled in an old farmhouse on land I owned that my family had once lived in. And I wrote my first novel, *Trees of Heaven,* which was accepted and published in 1940. In 1942, Jane, our only child, was born. And I wrote *Taps for Private Tussie,* which was published around the world and sold over two million copies. Then came World War II, in which I served in the U.S. Naval Reserve.

Before, during, and after the war, I had a book published most every year. Magazines bought my articles, stories, and poems, and paid good fees. I could have lived from lecture fees alone. In one year I gave eighty-seven lectures in thirty-three states. The world belonged to me. One major lecture per day was not enough. In Illinois one day I gave three, with a helicopter taking me from one to another. I often had a chartered plane to take me between two major lectures in a day. I was all man, all energy, couldn't be told or warned about burning the candle at both ends.

I fell at Murray State University, with a massive coronary, on October 8, 1954, after speaking to Kentucky's First District Teachers Association. A plane was waiting to take me to my second lecture at Flora, Illinois. I remained forty-eight days at the hospital there, and eleven months in bed at home. I had to learn to use my hands again. I had to learn to walk again. And I did grow back toenails, which I had lost. Now, I was a new man. I told this story in *The Year of My Rebirth.* I learned that money wasn't all. I was a lucky man to have lived, for my clothes weren't removed from my body for seven days after I fell in Murray.

16

Slowly I rebuilt a new world for myself and my family. I heard there was trouble at McKell High School, that it had "broken down in discipline," and in September 1957, my doctors agreed to let me try being principal. The story of this year, what transpired at McKell High School, is now legendary. A portion of what happened is in my book, *Mr. Gallion's School.* In the summer of 1968, Naomi, Jane, and I went to Reno, Nevada, to live. I taught in the Graduate College of Education of the University of Nevada, and with Naomi's help I taught a large creative writing class. This was a most productive summer.

In 1959 I was writing constantly and doing some lectures. In early 1960 I had more physical troubles and had to remain in an air-conditioned room. I can't forget this summer. Jane was now eighteen and she had finished at Stuart Hall Girls' School. She had arrived home from graduation and found me in my pajamas in this air-conditioned room. I'd read books. I'd written stories and articles. Naomi decided we should get our first TV set so I could watch ballgames. I had refused to have television in the house when Jane was growing up here. So we got our first television.

One day I answered a phone call.

"Is this Jesse Stuart?" said a man's voice.

"Yes, this is he!"

"This is Dr. Raymond McLain, president of American University in Cairo. I wonder if we can get the man who wrote *The Thread That Runs So True* to come here and teach for us."

"I'm confused about American University in Cairo," I said. "Where is it?"

"Cairo, Egypt," he replied. "I have friends in the States who have told me your health hasn't been too good here of late."

"My health is just fine," I said. "I'm over all the illnesses I've had. I'm ready to work again. And I think teaching in Egypt would be great. It would be a new experience."

Naomi wondered if I was right in wanting to go to Egypt. But I had that feeling that it was going to be all right. And Jane was eager for this journey. She would do her first year's work in an American university on foreign soil. Early summer we spent in preparation for a year or longer away from home.

Since Jane was an honor student in Latin, she planned to continue her studies in this subject. So we wanted to go early and take Jane over all of Italy, which had been the heart of the old Roman Empire. After this tour of Italy we would go on to Egypt and Cairo. Then, we promised Jane to take her over the countries the Romans once had in their empire on vacations from Cairo and after the teaching year was over. We'd take her all over Europe. And this we did. We spent most of the summer traveling after my teaching year was over.

My first speaking appearance in Cairo came about in an interesting way. When John Slocum was a young man he was on the editorial staff of *Scribner's* magazine. Later he became cultural attaché at the American embassy in Egypt. He remembered some of the material I had submitted to the magazine, and he knew my background. He asked me to speak at the embassy auditorium and to give a personal story, especially for those Egyptians who thought that all Americans were rich. Because I was from a rural Kentucky mountain family who had enjoyed a struggle, I could tell them of an American way of life they didn't know existed.

I told my students at American University, ones who expected grades from me, my young, eager, and ambitious students from many countries in other parts of Africa and the Near East as well as Egypt, that I was going to speak. I told them it would be important for them to come and bring their families. When I spoke, American embassy officials got a surprise. The auditorium, which seated 300 and had never been filled to capacity, was packed. Even the standing room was filled.

I wanted to surprise the audience with my beginning. "If I were an Egyptian," I said, "I would have been born in your poorest village." This, in Egypt, was unbelievable.

I never finished my talk about life in W-Hollow, about Plum Grove School and Greenup High School. I never even got to my college years and beyond. There was so much to tell them about my boyhood that I was behind the podium for two hours. When I finished there was a mad rush forward. I had reached this audience.

In addition to teaching at American University I spoke all over Egypt under the auspices of the American embassy. Egyptians were rioting against the United States, but they welcomed Jesse Stuart from W-Hollow.

Because of my success as a teacher and speaker in Egypt, I was sent around the world the next year by the United States Information Service, a part of our State Department. I returned to Egypt and when I finished there I was given a reception by the Egyptian State Department of Education. Our countries were not even friendly at that time, but I was in a position to invite some of the personnel of the American embassy to places where they had not been invited before. This raised eyebrows in some quarters. But I was accepted because the people felt that they could level with this W-Hollow man. I could level with their rural backgrounds and their efforts to build schools and upgrade education.

Shortly after I had finished my work around the world for the USIS, my book *God's Oddling* was published. From this book the USIS published excerpts which they entitled *Strength from the Hills*. They sent this book to countries around the world for use by people who were learning to read, write, and speak English.

God's Oddling was about my father, my mother, and our family. It told how we worked and struggled. Through its pages W-Hollow covered the world. My father never read a book. He never wrote a letter or read one. Intelligent as he was, he couldn't read or write. But the Stuarts of W-Hollow leveled with the world.

In my going around the world, working for the USIS, the "right arm" of our State Department, Naomi went with me. I paid all of her expenses from my salary. I didn't try to make money. And I didn't make money. I lost money.

In all of the first six countries we visited—Iran, Egypt, Greece, Lebanon, West Pakistan, and East Pakistan (now Bangladesh)—we found extremely poor people, too many of whom were illiterate because of the lack of educational opportunities. They just didn't have enough schools, except for Lebanon. I worked and spoke in dual professions: education and creative writing. In education I worked with secondary schools (of which there was a great lack), and Naomi, with fifteen years' experience as an elementary teacher, worked with elementary schools. She did a great work too.

Naomi had to leave me in Dacca, Bangladesh, for here she received the unfortunate news that her parents had been killed in an automobile accident. I went on alone by way of India, Burma, and Thailand, to the Philippines, Taiwan, and Korea. In all of these countries there were millions and millions of young, middle-aged, and older people struggling and looking for more education. I could work with them. Once I had been a small boy in W-Hollow with three sisters and a brother, whose father couldn't read and write and whose mother had a second grade education. I had been just as poor in my youth as these teeming millions in countries where I worked and struggled to help them. I wasn't in any country where I was ever called an "ugly American." The people loved me and Naomi and we loved the people. Many a night after working with the people in rural Greece (where youth are so bright), in East and West Pakistan, the Philippines (where they're really doing a job in education), and in Taiwan and Korea, after my long days were over I went to my room and cried. I wanted to lift these people to the skies. I wanted to lift them up to realms in an educated world where everything would be different for them, as it had been for me. "Learning is light and light is God," so Egyptians say. And they are right.

Education was that wonder sought, and after getting it, I found there was no way to measure how important it was to man. My tour for the USIS was considered the best and most successful one ever done by an individual. We had left home going east. I returned home from the west, a loser financially but a winner educationally in new experiences. I had given the biggest and best contribution of my lifetime. I came home and went directly to the hospital. I had given my all.

MY EAST KENTUCKY

AMERICA, all fifty states, is my land. Kentucky, so definitely my land, too, contains several states within its rugged, irregular boundaries. The East Kentucky mountain region is the part of Kentucky that has nurtured my people for a century and a half. They have breathed its fresh clean air, have eaten food from its soil, have seen the seasons come and go. They have lived their lives in this part of Kentucky, though many of the young have moved on to other states, mostly Ohio, for better opportunities. Now, many of the Kentuckians from my area who moved away for better opportunities in Ohio are moving back here for better opportunities in Kentucky. With an energy problem in America, coal is energy and the mining industry is booming.

This state within Kentucky, the hilly section with its narrow-gauged valleys and swift rivers and streams, is referred to as the Eastern Kentucky Coal Fields, but this is not an adequate name. True, coal is our main product. Kentucky produces more coal than West Virginia or Pennsylvania or any other state in the union. But we are something more than one of the top coal-producing areas of the country. We should be referred to as the East Kentucky mountains.

My East Kentucky mountain area, with the exception of

Pine Mountain and Cumberland Mountain, is known to geologists as the Cumberland Plateau. Its mountains and valleys were not created by powerful forces in the earth's interior, as most mountains are, but by erosion of a high plateau. Notice the horizontal layers of rock. They are a geologist's dream, for they give a vertical profile of the geologic ages of this region. It is not uncommon to see a car with a foreign license parked along one of our highways where the road has been cut through layer after layer of stone. Men will be out with small picks, writing pads, and cameras. They park, too, where a highway is close to the side of a steep cliff which shows these rock strata all the way from the narrow valley bottom to the top.

Pull out a map of Kentucky and draw a line on it. Begin the line where the hills end and the Bluegrass begins, where Lewis and Mason counties meet. Let the line bear southwest at about a 15° angle and it will emerge somewhere near Albany, Kentucky, and the Tennessee state line. East of this line lies an area the size of Vermont or a little larger. It is approximately 10,500 square miles, roughly one-fourth the area of Kentucky. Oil, gas, and iron ore are found here, but not abundantly. In Harlan County stands Big Black Mountain, its peak 4,145 feet above sea level, the highest point in the state. Certainly this area is above all else "coal country." Coal is produced in all its counties, though with only a limited amount in Lewis County, the most northerly and one of the most scenic in Appalachia.

Despite the value of East Kentucky's coal, I firmly believe that what is on top of the ground is as valuable as, perhaps more valuable than, what lies under the ground. The exploitation of what lies under our ground may diminish what lies on top in years to come. But if we protect our soil, our water, our natural resources, they will be with us for millenniums. In East Kentucky we have mountains and hills as beautiful as any in the world. They produce poets as well as coal miners. Our Kentucky state parks, among the nation's finest, are bringing tourists from all over the United States to see this great natural beauty.

Drive up our Big Sandy River and its Levisa Fork to Prestonsburg, oldest settlement in the Big Sandy Valley, and Pikeville, once a lumbering as well as a coal center, and on beyond to the Breaks. You will encounter scenery unlike any other in America. This wild, steep country, with its hairpin-curved roads, will make you wonder how pioneers ever reached it. They came on foot and on horseback from Virginia, the Carolinas, and the eastern seaboard, through Pound Gap, prior to 1800. They came down into the Big Sandy Valley and spread inland, settling in the Kentucky mountains. They went down to the Ohio River Valley and across the Ohio River into the Midwest.

Consider what my early ancestors found when they came in this way between 1790 and 1820. Mountains and valleys were filled with hardwood and softwood timber: red oaks, white oaks, black oaks, ash, maple, yellow pines, and white and yellow poplars. The world they found looked as if it might have been freshly created. Riffles of clean, cool, mountain water cascaded down the slopes and ran swiftly down the valleys. This was water unpolluted, fit for drinking by wildlife, domestic animals, and man. There was surface water in plenty and water from springs, for this was before streams of sulphur water from coal seams had been tapped by miners.

Not long ago Naomi and I drove south on U.S. Route 23 along the Big Sandy and Levisa Fork to beyond Pikeville with our friends Ben and Jean Webb. The Big Sandy Valley was the home of my pioneer ancestors and those of the Webbs. Some of our ancestors sleep in Lawrence, Johnson, Floyd, and Pike counties.

We left Route 23 near Shelbiana, in the heart of Pike County, the largest and the greatest coal-producing county in Kentucky. Here we began our climb over a hairpin-curved mountain road that would take us up to Breaks Interstate Park, which lies in both Kentucky and Virginia. We were heading up among the clouds. On the way we stopped and looked down into Breaks Canyon. Water riffled over rocks, with spray leaping up like flying silverfish in the sun. As we drove on slowly among breathtaking scenes, Naomi and I were reminded of landscapes we had seen at Grimsel and Firka passes in Switzerland.

We reached Breaks Interstate Park and settled into our rooms. We had no air conditioning or telephones. We didn't need either, up here in this land of the sky, this Switzerland of Kentucky. Our rooms were on the rim of the canyon, one of the deepest east of the Mississippi. Below us flowed singing waters that lulled us to sleep at night.

We stayed here four nights. Each morning as we got up we could still hear the waters rushing along down there in the canyon, but we couldn't see the water. A white cloud floor blotted out the canyon until the sun rose high enough to evaporate it. Often mountain peaks would jut up through the clouds, reminding me of uninhabitable islands I had seen thrusting up through the waters of the Mediterranean Sea. None of the other regions of Kentucky has a scene like this.

I have said that there is something more to our mountains than their being loaded from bottom to pinnacle with seams of coal. These Cumberland Mountains are more beautiful than the Alps because of their seasonal changes. They are never snow-capped for long. And even on their tops they are covered with hardwood forest, making them among the most scenic in the world in all four seasons. They're not the highest mountains in the world, but they are unique in their formation of ridges and pinnacles, in their sunlit rivers, zigzagging like gigantic silver snakes down the narrow valleys where there is little farmland, hardly enough level space for rows of houses.

At Breaks Interstate Park you can stand, as we have often done, and see the morning sun like a giant red cartwheel reach its dazzling splinters to touch each mountain top and ridge. Slowly the sun's fingers penetrate each deep, dark, morning valley where shadows and mists mix and mingle. The best way to know this park in early morning is to have a pre-breakfast before the real breakfast. First on the menu, enjoy bowls of bright morning sunlight to nourish the spirit and stir inspiration. Let the good food to nourish the body come later. Draw breath deeply into your lungs! In the morning at the Breaks I stand on my toes and rock back on my heels and breathe this invigorating air into my lungs. It is like standing in the beginning of the world.

Of course, there is danger in this world, too. This is the home of the rattlesnake and the copperhead and once it was home of the bear and wolf. A little story I remember illustrates the tenacity of the mountain woman. One morning a woman took her bucket and went to pick wild huckleberries where they grew profusely along the mountain ridges. She didn't come home at the time she was expected, so her husband went to look for her. When he found her, with her bucket half-filled with huckleberries, she was lying dead on the ground. But her assassin was also dead. She had choked the rattlesnake that had bitten her and she was still holding him in a death grip.

Almost everyone in the nation is aware of our mountain feuds. In earlier years our habit of "taking the law into our own hands" became legendary. The gun was the law then as it is today in the Khyber Pass area of West Pakistan. But at the Breaks Park, danger and guns seem far away. Days that begin with sunlight splintering along the mountain peaks end with dazzling sunsets. Once when I was on the west coast of Florida, I was told that the sunsets there are extraordinary. Artists living there assured me their sunsets aren't equaled anywhere in the world. I quickly replied that they would have to be great ones to compare with those I had seen in two other places: the Greek Isles and Breaks Interstate Park in Pike County, Kentucky.

Coming home from different parts of America I used to fly over these East Kentucky mountains. I seldom fly over them any more. I prefer surface travel where I don't have to look down on the grievous scars defacing some of our mountains. Many of these will never be healed. One mountain I have seen has a ring cut completely around its top, like an old man who has had his hair cut crock-style. It stands, an eyesore and an object of pity, amidst the beauty of surrounding mountains.

To drive from Pike County north along the Levisa Fork and the Big Sandy and then along the broad, majestic Ohio is to follow one of the most scenic drives in America. Willows and silver maples and cottonwoods line the banks along the Ohio. When you arrive at the line dividing Lewis and Mason counties, you will have driven from extreme south to north along the most eastern route in the East Kentucky mountains.

Another magnificent sight is the great mountain pass, one of the most famous in America, made familiar around the world in song and story: Cumberland Gap. Through this gap Daniel Boone came with his party into Kentucky. Settlers from Virginia, North Carolina, and the eastern seaboard came this way by the thousands: men, women, and children, with their horses and mules, their hogs, cattle, geese, and turkeys. After passing through Cumberland Gap, they fanned out on wilderness trails to other parts of this unsettled land. Most moved north into the Bluegrass country and farther west toward Louisville, or westward across the southern part of Kentucky, through the "Pennyrile" district into the good farmland of western Kentucky and the Jackson Purchase. Many of these pioneers moved on to Arkansas, Missouri, Kansas, Oklahoma, and California, following the sunset. This group included our greatest pioneer, Daniel Boone. He moved on to Missouri, where he died. But Kentuckians couldn't let his dust remain anywhere outside this state. They brought his remains back to Frankfort, our capital city.

When I was in college at Lincoln Memorial University at Harrogate, Tennessee, in 1926, we students used to walk the mile from our campus to the gap and observe the steep road with its wagon ruts still running down the hill into the little town of Cumberland Gap. At that time automobiles needed good engines and brakes to drive from Harrogate up and over the gap. It was hard to imagine how difficult it must have been for the pioneers to cross here and through Pound Gap. They had to be rugged people. But once they saw the beauty of this new land and all its opportunities, nothing could make them turn back to their peaceful settlements in Virginia and the Carolinas. They defied Indians, panthers, wolves, bears, copperheads, rattlesnakes, and many other foes.

The mountain region they found is still my land today. It is mine in all seasons. In April, my favorite month, everything seems young in Kentucky. Dogwoods, redbuds, wild crab apples, and plums scatter white and pink blooms which are blown by the wind in the valleys and on the slopes of the hills. The earth in April seems alive with white-hair roots and the trees are filled with the growing green-hair. In July, the sun is as hot as a roasted potato. The wind, in dry burning sheets, moves slowly over the land and rubs the dry bellies of the poplar leaves until their green throats rattle. Then in winter, there are great nights in the woods when hounds run and millions of white stars overhead hang high, high over the bony ridges where the foxes raise their young in holes under the great rocks.

I have told about this land and its pioneers in forty-five of our fifty states and in countries around the world. At the University of Alexandria, in Egypt, where the good doctor Luke used to teach medicine, my speeches were so convincing that students followed me to the gate of the university. They begged me to help them get to America and to Kentucky so they could live as I had lived. The

28

same was true in all the countries where I spoke. The majority of the youth in these countries spoke what is called "England's English." They liked my English. They didn't call it "American English" but "Kentucky English." I needed a translator in only two of nine countries where I spoke, Iran and Korea.

But the finest compliment I ever received on my English was at the Bread Loaf Writers Conference at Bread Loaf Mountain, Vermont. Robert Frost was in the audience. After I had finished my lecture, he came up to me and said, "Where did you get that kind of English you've used?" I knew that Frost was a humorous man and I wondered if he was kidding me.

"It's the kind we speak down in the East Kentucky mountains and hills," I said. "It's the only language I know."

"It's the strongest and best English I've heard spoken in many a year," he said, with a smile. "Your idiomatic expressions and your language are strong. It's the type of English that should be spoken." He had made notes of some of the words I had used. I have often wished since that I had asked to see the words he wrote down. I wish he had given me the envelope on which he had made his notes.

One of my former students at McKell High School in Greenup County, Monnie Roe, later graduated from Morehead State College and went to teach high school English in a mountain county not far from Morehead. She found it difficult for her students to understand stories in their textbooks, for they were written in American English. Later she did a study at Peabody College in Nashville on the Middle English words still used by young people in the East Kentucky mountains.

I know that we of the East Kentucky mountains have a slightly different way of writing and speaking. We have had education and travel, have participated in two global wars, and have listened daily to radio and television, but we have never lost our distinctive language. This is true for the English in certain parts of England, too, for the Welsh in Wales, for the Scots of Scotland, and the Irish of Ireland. There are still different dialects associated with distinctive sections in their countries.

In this mountain region of Kentucky, this Appalachian world, I know that I was born in the right place at the right time.

MY BLUEGRASS

I CAN CHANGE WORLDS in two hours in Kentucky. All I have to do is drive up scenic Route 1, along the Little Sandy (a river and an area that remind me of following the Tiber out of Rome) and arrive at Interstate 64 at Grayson. From Grayson I follow I-64 westward across East Kentucky's high hills and Knobs. Without speed limits this could be a fast road. But who wants to drive fast along this scenic route? Better to go slower and see the cliffs, the hardwood trees, the tough-butted white oaks that hold their leaves in winter, the sawbriars and blackberry briars, old fences, old houses, country cemeteries, valleys, and streams. This is a country where stubborn people cling tenaciously to their stubborn soil.

Now in an hour and a half, just beyond Morehead, we drive into the Outer Bluegrass world. Here everything is different. Here we find excellent cattle farms, and tobacco barns painted black with red roofs. Here we see evidence of wealth spread over the land and the buildings. These are farms where farmers can make money and not have to be subsidized by the federal government. And what makes the difference? Soil! Here we reach the limestone soil. People from the East driving this way often park their cars off the Interstate 64 concrete and bring out their cameras. But this is only the beginning.

They are not yet in the heart of the Bluegrass country, with Lexington as its capital city. They will have to have more film.

There is an Inner Bluegrass country which is approximately the size of Rhode Island, and an Outer Bluegrass country the approximate size of Massachusetts. Together with the so-called Eden Shale belt, these cover about 9,000 square miles to form the famous Bluegrass country of Kentucky. It is a beautiful, original land, the best-known section of the state. This region was described by Elizabeth Madox Roberts, in a novel of early pioneer days, as *The Great Meadow*. It was so called by the Indians.

And on the present site of Winchester, Kentucky, near Lexington, there was an Indian village by the name of Iskipakathiki. Isn't this an extraordinary and beautiful word? This name is Shawnee and its meaning is "the place where it's green all over." From prehistoric days to the present the Inner Bluegrass must have been the Eden of the North American continent.

Lexington, at its heart, is now the fastest growing city in Kentucky. It was once called the Athens of the West. Certainly it is the Athens of Kentucky, with its University of Kentucky and Transylvania University. The latter was the first college founded west of the Alleghenies. Established by Presbyterians in 1782, Transylvania had as one of its early professors of Greek and Latin the Reverend Robert Stuart, a Presbyterian minister and an ancestor of mine.

Lexington is a city I like. It has a character all its own. I hope that the old Phoenix Hotel downtown and the area around it will not be destroyed by some urban renewal project. Here was the beginning of culture in this important city. Here great and near-great Kentuckians of an earlier day walked and talked. Here the gentry of early Kentucky made local, state, and national history.

The country around Lexington, with its black or white board fences and palatial homes set in a background of rolling green fields, is more beautiful than many of America's well-kept parks. The Inner Bluegrass would be a showplace even in Japan, Germany, France, or Switzerland, where land is carefully and beautifully tended. Lexington and Paris and other Bluegrass towns have many of the characteristics of English cities and towns. In fact, many Bluegrass towns are named for their counterparts in England: Winchester, Lancaster, Richmond.

I have spoken at the University of Kentucky during the administrations of four different presidents. Naomi and I have spent time in their homes. Breakfasts at the president's home, Maxwell Place, are like the hearty English breakfasts we were served when we stayed at English inns which advertised "bed and breakfast." They are similar, too, to the breakfasts served by old New England families we have known.

I have traveled through England and seen the clean farms with cattle, sheep, and horses enclosed by rock fences. I have explored the narrow, winding, tree-shaded roads and seen fine farmhouses and barns. Our Bluegrass offers the same sights. No wonder Bluegrass people and English people visit each other and have so much in common. The early settlers of the Bluegrass and the English were just a step apart; perhaps, not so much as a step, in their social divisions. This was and is (to a lesser extent today) typical of the Bluegrass people. No wonder it is a little difficult for the East Kentucky mountaineer, who is far removed from any desire for an aristocracy, to understand the people here.

My people of the mountains of East Kentucky are as different from the people of the Bluegrass as day is from night. I think of my friend J. Winston Coleman, the "Squire of the Bluegrass." He is an authority on this area and has captured it in pictures and stories. Could he ever be content to live in the mountains of East Kentucky or any other section of this state? He would be lost! His people have lived in the Bluegrass since 1800. There are many other old families in this inner core.

33

What has given our Bluegrass of Kentucky an international reputation? The attraction has been twofold: the Kentucky Thoroughbred and Kentucky bourbon. What Scotch whiskey is to Scotland, bourbon whiskey is to Kentucky. Kentucky produces seven-eighths of the bourbon distilled in the world. The combination of fine whiskey and fine horseflesh reaches a pinnacle of perfection that draws visitors from all corners of the world on Derby Day at Churchill Downs. The Derby is run in Louisville, but many of the horses are bred on Bluegrass farms and the mint juleps are made with bourbon distilled with the limestone water of the Bluegrass region.

But there is more to our Bluegrass country than horse farms, race tracks, and bourbon whiskey. These are just parts, albeit famous parts. This limestone land grows the finest burley tobacco in the world. In summer the fields of tobacco bloom, and in autumn the leaves turn a deep gold. Kentucky produces nearly two-thirds of the burley tobacco raised in the United States, and Lexington, with its enormous tobacco warehouses, is the burley center of Kentucky. This is air-dried tobacco, hung in fine boxed and painted barns with occasional cracks left between the planks so the wind can blow through and dry the tobacco naturally. How different these fine barns are from many of those in my East Kentucky mountains, where even boxed barns are seldom painted. Many of our barns are made of posts tied together with braces and poles, so the tobacco is protected from the weather only on the top.

With the exception of the Jackson Purchase area, the Bluegrass is the finest farmland in Kentucky. Fine corn, wheat, oats, hay, and barley are grown here. Little wonder that farmhouses and barns here are among the best in America. This land produces wealth.

The rolling hills of the Bluegrass area support cattle, sheep, and hogs, as well as horses. Many breeds of cattle graze peacefully in its lush bluegrass pastures, where lonely, gigantic oaks extend their great arms to the incessant wind, and little streams flow silver in the sunlight.

Unfortunately streams often sink in this limestone land. Livestock must often be watered from man-made lakes and ponds.

I often park beside a farm and watch hundreds of sheep grazing peacefully, as I have watched sheep on farms in Scotland, along the North Sea and up in Caithness. I shall never forget the images of gray woolly sheep dotting that cool green land. I return to the Bluegrass of Kentucky to revive these memories, as well as memories of the sheep I used to raise on my farm.

But there are differences between Scotland and the Bluegrass. One needs to get up a bit closer to the gray limestone rocks that lie scattered over Bluegrass fields. A tourist might think these are sheep lying down for a rest. How many times I have been fooled! One never sees these gray rocks in the sheep country of Scotland. The stone farmhouses in Scotland are mostly white, while Bluegrass farmhouses are of stone, brick, or wood, in a variety of colors. Unlike dour, misty, shadowy Scotland and England, Kentucky has plenty of sunshine in all seasons except winter.

The Thoroughbreds raised on the horse farms around Lexington are magnificent. Young colts, galloping over the green fields, playing in the wind and sun, while their mothers keep watch, will soon be in races. Some may be Derby contenders, cheered on to the finish by thousands of spectators. They will run in Kentucky, New York, and Maryland, and in England, France, Japan, South America, New Zealand, and Australia. Race horses for the world are bred here.

In my earlier years, when I first visited the University of Kentucky, Dr. Frank McVey was president. He was a very tall man, originally from North Dakota. His wife, Frances Jewell McVey, was a native Bluegrass woman. She too was large, attractive, and intelligent. Once she invited me to speak in Lexington to the Association of American University Women. After the talk I remarked to her about the height of these women.

"They are tall and active," she replied. "If we continue to eat foods grown from this soil, we'll produce tall and large people. It is said that Kentucky horses nourished on bluegrass, barley, oats, hay, and corn grown on this Bluegrass soil have an extra stamina and endurance. Check the track records of Kentucky-bred horses with the records of horses bred and grown in other areas and see the difference!"

Any drive over any road in the Outer Bluegrass is good to take. But I like the drive from Lexington to Maysville up on the Ohio River to see the cattle, sheep, and farm country. This is more scenic than Scotland's two most comparable areas, around Callander and in the Lowlands.

On the western rim of the Outer Bluegrass is Bardstown, founded in 1775, one of the earliest permanent settlements in Kentucky. At this tourist mecca is Federal Hill, more widely familiar as My Old Kentucky Home. Here legend says that Stephen Foster wrote the song "My Old Kentucky Home." And here is Saint Joseph's Cathedral, built in 1820, a magnet for thousands of Catholic pilgrims and non-Catholic visitors each year. If one has not eaten here at ancient Talbot Inn, most famous in Kentucky, then he has missed something of the past and of the present.

The Inner and Outer Bluegrass areas of Kentucky could well be a separate state. When I visit this fabulous land I try to adjust myself mentally for the experience. Even the language is different here. I learned this on my first visit to the Bluegrass when I was a young man. I learned, also, about the different levels of society in the Bluegrass. Even among the horse people there are differences between those who raise trotting horses or pacers and those who raise Thoroughbreds. It is a great way of life here among the affluent farmers and business people in the Inner Bluegrass area. No wonder the people of my East Kentucky mountains move up to the Bluegrass area for better opportunities.

There has been, and maybe there still is, a great movement of mountaineers from my East Kentucky mountain counties south of the Bluegrass up to Lexington, Winchester, Paris, and all over the inner and outer areas of this fabulous land. Many migrated here as tenant farmers. Many came for work in industry, for industries now flourish in the Lexington and Winchester areas. Many who made money in coal have come here and purchased farms. Many from New York State and New England have purchased farms here as well as a few from foreign countries. Now with the energy problem in the United States bringing a greater demand for coal, this migration of mountaineers to the Bluegrass may well slow down.

This, then, is my Bluegrass world: parklike horse farms; cattle, sheep, and tobacco farms; homes and colleges that represent a high standard of life; land inviting contentment.

> . . . *The heart of America*
> *A land of even tempo,*
> *A land of mild traditions,*
> *A land that has kept its tradition of horse racing,*
> *Ballad, song, story and folk music.*
> *It has held steadfast to its pioneer tradition*
> *Of fighting men, fighting for America*
> *And for the soil of Kentucky,*
> *That is filled with bluegrass beauty*
> *That is not akin to poetry*
> *But is poetry . . . .*
> *And when I go beyond the border,*
> *I take with me growth and beauty of the seasons,*
> *The music of wind in pine and cedar tops,*
> *The wordless songs of snow-melted water*
> *When it pours over the rocks to wake the spring.*
> *I take with me Kentucky embedded in my brain*
> *   and heart,*
> *In my flesh and bone and blood*
> *Since I am of Kentucky*
> *And Kentucky is part of me.*

MY KNOBS COUNTRY

HERE IS A REGION I call Haystacks Tapering to the Sky. It is a singular part of Kentucky's varied and changeable landscape.

The Knobs country begins at West Point, about twenty miles southwest of Louisville. Stretching from ten to thirty miles wide, it forms a semicircle like a giant horseshoe around the Inner and Outer Bluegrass areas. In Indiana the Knobs area bends slightly northwest, as if it is trying to go back and connect with its beginning and thus form a complete circle.

In this belt of unusual geographical formations the hills go up like volcanic cones or haystacks, with narrow valleys between. Daniel Boone and his followers, who discovered this region, found buffalo and deer grazing here. In these winding valleys between cone-shaped hills were canebrakes where these animals fed in all seasons, especially in the winter. It was here that pioneers came to get their meat for winter. Today the buffalo are extinct, the deer are scarce, and the canebrakes in the strips of flatlands between the Knobs are practically gone. These flat areas now grow corn, tobacco, sorghum cane, and hay. This flatland also provides good pasture for domestic animals.

The slopes of the Knobs, except in rare instances down near their bases, are too steep to be farmed or used as pasture. Cattle could not stand on the higher slopes. I even doubt if goats could maneuver on the steeps of these cone-shaped hills.

I first became aware of the Knobs when I was sixteen, riding a troop train through Ohio, Indiana, and Louisville, and down to Fort Knox. I was on my way to the Citizens Military Training Camp (CMTC), which was at Fort Knox. I had never even heard of the Knobs. South of Louisville, I saw these unusual hills, standing out there like small pyramids, hills that seemed out of place. From Fort Knox a number of us with tents, blankets, and food returned to the Knobs for an unforgettable weekend.

On the level land between cones, in the deep valleys, are farmhouses and barns. These are different from the ones in the Bluegrass area, the Jackson Purchase, or even the valleys of the East Kentucky mountains. Many of the early log houses in the Knobs region were built with two front doors, leading to two rooms of equal importance, a front living room for visitors and a parlor where only special guests were invited and young people did their courting. In a large house there would be more rooms behind these, perhaps a dining room behind the parlor, and still farther back a kitchen and back porch. Some had upstairs rooms over the living room and parlor. In a smaller house with two doors there would be no upstairs rooms, and an L would run back from the living room with a dining room and kitchen.

In my East Kentucky mountains in approximately the same period, there were homes everywhere made of logs, and later boxed houses with an open hallway, called a "dog trot," between the two front rooms. One of these was usually a sitting room and one was a parlor. Overhead were bedrooms. Behind the sitting room and parlor was usually a dining room, and behind this a kitchen and back porch. The people used the front of the "dog trot" as a porch when they wanted to sit out. In my youth these houses were all over this area. Now one scarcely can be found. The house where we live now used to have a "dog trot."

Barns in the Knobs region in earlier years were either of logs or boxed, as in other regions of the state. There was usually a large double door. A wagonload of hay could be pulled in through the lower door and forked through the upper door into the hayloft. We have some few small barns in our mountain area like this now. In other regions of the state barns often had a sliding door at either end and a broad hallway through the middle of the barn, with cattle, horse, and mule stanchions on either side. But early simple architecture of the Knobs had its own distinctive character.

A traveler driving from Lexington to Elizabethtown on the Bluegrass Parkway crosses the Knobs country. When he sees that chain of low mountains looming up before him, those conical hills, green in summer or multicolored in autumn or barren of leaves in deep winter, standing like lonely sentinels, hand-carved and placed there in a methodical row by mythical giants, if he is any observer at all, with a love of nature, he will pull his car over to the side of the interstate. Then he will sit, observe, and wonder. I have seen tourists do this at one particularly scenic spot. A stream, six to ten feet wide, runs between the interstate and the chain of haystack mountains. It flows lazily between the summer cornfields, tobacco patches, meadows, and pastures, and fades into the distance between two hills that seem to be reaching up for more light from the sun.

Driving here, Naomi and I have seen sunsets like those along the Greek Isles in the Mediterranean. There the sun goes down very fast and seems to fall with a plop into the blue waters, down to Poseidon, the god of the sea. Our Kentucky sunset, viewed from the Knobs, moves swiftly, too, and drops down, down, down in the far west, dragging a patch of red clouds behind it.

Naomi and I, driving along this route, have parked many times where the tourists park. Here I have made notes for poems and stored up mental pictures to use in years to come. And I have wished that travelers from around the world could see this strange and fascinating wonderland.

Jimmy Norris, Sr., co-owner and editor emeritus of the *Ashland Daily Independent*, sat with me one noon at the coffee table in the Henry Clay House, where Ashland business and professional men meet for lunch. Our conversation turned to the Knobs country. Jimmy is an astute student of Kentucky's history, its topography and diversified beauty, its sections, which he knows and has observed closely in his eighty years.

"Jesse," he said, "the Knobs area of Kentucky is one of the most unusual geographical formations in this state, in the United States, in the world, I presume. Geologists have never quite figured this one out. I remember when I was a young man at Centre College our class went in wagons down to the Knobs for an overnight stay. One of the things I remember, besides the unusual beauty of the place, was the way in which we would strike matches and throw them on the ground and there would be a bright flame. We did this in the dark. The sulphur content in the ground there is so great it caused this extra flame from the match. I used to drive out of my way to see this chain of volcanic-shaped hills, which seem to sit upon the surface of Kentucky without any reason for being there."

But, I thought, back in the beginnings of time, there was some reason for the Knobs being here, a reason that has never been satisfactorily understood and explained.

Why is an area like the Knobs, a place of such unusual beauty, less known than other regions of the state? Not another place in the world offers such uncommon physical formations. Perhaps one reason the Knobs are so little known is that no road follows them from West Point in a semicircle eastward to Morehead and onward to the Ohio River. Such a road would be expensive and difficult to build. There are short roads running parallel to the Knobs, and roads crossing them at scattered points through gaps where roadbuilding is less expensive. But if a scenic route followed this long, narrow Knobs country, it would be traveled by millions as one of Kentucky's scenic wonders.

Another reason may be the competition from other parts of Kentucky so conspicuously famous. Then, too, this quarter-moon-shaped strip of land is two hundred miles long. Kentucky's other sections are compact and easily comprehended; they have good roads, state parks, and tourist accommodations. But not the Knobs.

This Knobs country has been exceedingly fortunate in one respect, however. It has had a great writer to immortalize it: Elizabeth Madox Roberts, who was born in 1886 in Perryville and died in 1941. She resided as an adult in Springfield, Kentucky. A well-educated writer and a teacher, she wrote one novel now considered a minor classic, *The Time of Man*. In this book, Ellen Chesser grows from childhood to womanhood; she is first the daughter and then the wife of a tenant farmer. Her family is always close to the land but never has any acres to call its own. Ellen Chesser is one of the great characters in fiction. I doubt if a greater novel has been written by a Kentuckian. *The Time of Man* was one of the books selected for reading in the novel course taught by Robert Penn Warren when I was a student at Vanderbilt.

Miss Roberts published ten other books. These poem and short story collections and novels depict her area of Kentucky in her day and time. In *The Time of Man* she presents a portrait of a Knobs family struggling with the poor soil to eke out a scanty living. This is a beautiful book about close-to-earth people, a novel akin to poetry.

After reading *The Time of Man* I was eager to meet Elizabeth Madox Roberts. This opportunity came when we were in Louisville at the same time. We talked about her short stories, her poetry, and her novels. But we especially discussed *The Time of Man*. She gave me directions so that I could locate the setting of her book, an area that I later went to see.

Kentucky remains the number one state in the nation for its number of fine parks and lodges to go with them for the thousands of tourists from over America and the world. Tourism from these parks is Kentucky's third largest source of income. These fine Kentucky parks are too numerous to mention in this book. It would take a much larger book to describe them, but there is one unusual park in the Knobs region, Bernheim Forest, which is not a state or a national park. It is owned and operated by the Isaac Bernheim Foundation "for the use and benefit of the people of Kentucky and their friends." It receives no tax support.

Bernheim Forest, near Louisville and four miles south of Shepherdsville, is 10,000 acres of rural enchantment for thousands and thousands of visitors. When the late Isaac Bernheim purchased this land in 1923, it was an abused land, cut-over timber and wornout farms. Now see the forests growing there! Now see the plants, shrubs and trees from many foreign lands transplanted here.

Here is one of the finest wildlife sanctuaries in Kentucky. Fishermen are permitted to fish in both of its lakes, Lake Nevin and Cedar Lake, but they are not permitted to use live minnows for bait! This gives you an idea about the respect here for wildlife. I have never used a live minnow for bait in my life. There are roads where people, many who cannot walk, can drive through and see this park. There are endless paths for walking. There are facilities all over the area for cooking and picnicking. Mr. Isaac Bernheim left a living dream for multitudes of people to enjoy, perhaps as long as there is a Kentucky. What a great nature benefactor he has been to humanity. It is unfortunate that this far-seeing man couldn't or didn't buy up more of the old denuded acres. Each section of Kentucky needs a park like Bernheim Forest.

I wonder: What could and would people in other countries do if they were fortunate enough to have a formation like the Knobs on their land? I think of Italy with so many mountains and steep slopes. Farmers there cultivate land that seems too steep to farm, even steeper than the hill slopes we used to tend in the East Kentucky mountains, where we dug places ahead to stand on while we hoed the crops. These slopes we tended only with hoes. Not even a sure-footed mule could have stood to pull a plow. Italians do the same. I have watched men and women working on the sharp hillsides in Italy. But not even they could farm the Knobs. Not even East Kentucky mountaineers in our earlier years could have farmed the steep slopes of these hills. Not even the Swiss or the Norwegians, who farm and pasture steep land, could handle these precipitous angles. Their sheep and goats couldn't traverse these slopes.

There is only one thing to be done with the Knobs, these Haystacks Tapering to the Sky. These conical hills are here for the eye to see, the brain to comprehend, the imagination to appreciate.

MY PENNYROYAL

THE PENNYROYAL is a hodgepodge state in Kentucky, with vague borders. On the east it is bounded by the East Kentucky mountains. On the west it borders the Jackson Purchase and the Ohio River. On the north it wraps itself around the Western Coal Field and reaches to the Knobs. On the south it shares a common line with Tennessee. This Pennyroyal section borders all Kentucky sections but one—the Bluegrass. It embraces some 11,000 square miles.

Is it royal Pennyroyal or unroyal Pennyrile? The name comes from a plant abundant in this area. This little plant has a distinctive odor, pleasant to many, unpleasant to some. It grows all over Kentucky. Pennyrile is especially prolific in the East Kentucky mountains. As a child I used to gather pennyrile and carry it around with me to smell.

One way to describe this unusual section of the state is to say that it is an area with three panhandles. One extends northward between the Western Coal Field and the Knobs to the Ohio River. This is rock and cedar country. Then there is the western panhandle, jutting up between the Western Coal Field and the Jackson Purchase, reaching again to the Ohio River, with more cedar and rock country but with fewer hills and better farmlands. These two giant panhandles appear on the map to be standing up straight like the horns on a big Texas bull so large he could paw the earth and shake the water. The third panhandle is the eastern one, between the Knobs and the East Kentucky mountain area, reaching to include Somerset.

No wonder a stranger driving from Louisville to Paducah across the Knobs, then across the northern panhandle of the Pennyroyal, rock and cedar country, then into the western coal country, then into the western panhandle of the Pennyroyal, cedar and rock country again, and on into the fertile, level farmland of the Jackson Purchase, covering all of this in three hours—no wonder the stranger might become confused. If he stops and talks to the people, if he is sensitive to language and dialects, he will notice changes in both.

Nine of the Pennyroyal's big southern counties extend along the Tennessee border: Trigg, Christian, Todd, Logan, Simpson, Allen, Monroe, Cumberland, and Clinton. To the north of Simpson County is Warren County, with Bowling Green, the capital city of the Pennyroyal. The contrast between the two cities of Somerset and Bowling Green is striking. Somerset is the seat of Pulaski County and has been called the "Gateway to the Mountains." Bowling Green, seat of Warren County, is on the floodplain of the Barren River. Bowling Green has been noted for its asphalt rock from the Barren River, burley tobacco, and a strawberry market once the foremost in the state. Western Kentucky University is also here.

The Hill Top in Bowling Green was fortified by cannon during the Civil War. From this vantage point today a visitor can look in all directions. All highways in western Kentucky lead to Bowling Green. It has a good airport and good railroad facilities. It is a crossroads for travel from east to west and north to south. No wonder industry is booming here. Bowling Green, once the Confederate capital of Kentucky, is definitely capital of the Pennyroyal state.

To experience this part of the Pennyroyal, drive east on Route 68 from the Jackson Purchase through Hopkinsville, Russellville, and on to Bowling Green. Here you will find some of the finest farmland not only in Kentucky but in America. I prefer to drive here in summer when corn is maturing, wheat is turning from green to gold, and soybeans are high. This central Pennyroyal should be classified culturally with the Jackson Purchase. The people have a dialect similar to that of the Jackson Purchase people.

Driving across this area when corn is in full tassel and the ears are shooting multicolored silks on dark green stalks reminds me of traveling through the cornfield areas in western Ohio, Indiana, Illinois, Iowa, and Nebraska, and along the Nile River in Egypt, except for two things. In our midwestern states the barns are large and red, sometimes finer than the farm homes. In this area of Kentucky there are good barns all right, but also old plantation homes similar to those in Mississippi and Louisiana. This part of the Pennyroyal belongs to the Old South. Before Emancipation, thousands of Negro slaves worked these fertile and extensive farms, more evidence that there is a part of Kentucky that corresponds in some way to almost every part of the United States.

In the Pennyroyal's northwestern panhandle, close to the Knobs, I spent some time when I was sixteen and later at nineteen soldiering at Fort Knox. Fort Knox, and the gold of America which is stored there, bring in servicemen and their wives, as well as tourists, from all over America. On long marches, carrying a sixty-pound pack, I observed the land and its vegetation: pennyrile, sassafras, sawbriars, broomsedge, greenbriars, blackberry briars, and black and red sumacs (pronounced "shoe-makes" by many). Often I was hot and weary almost to the point of exhaustion as we marched over the old fields around Fort Knox. Sometimes, crossing country bridges, we had to get out of regular marching step so that our platoon wouldn't break the bridges down. I remember Muldraughs Hill and the rifle range to which we marched for practice. There I put many a bullet through the bull's-eye in all firing positions. I was a "sharpshooter" and lacked only one point of making "expert rifleman." I begged my officer to give it to me but he wouldn't concede the gift of a point, even after all the time I had lain on that rough earth of the Pennyroyal!

Twenty-eight miles northeast of Bowling Green is Mammoth Cave, largest cavern in the world, discovered in about 1799. My first visit there was when I was sixteen, and I have returned twice since, first to take my wife Naomi, and later to take our daughter Jane. We saw the great chamber, called Chief City, 450 feet long and 175 feet wide. When Naomi and I were there earlier we were impressed, as other visitors have been, by passages crowded with beautiful stalactites and stalagmites occurring in fantastic forms, resembling natural objects and architectural designs. Lakes, rivers, waterfalls, and fountains enhance the beauty of this subterranean scenery. Echo and Styx rivers and even the blind fish here fascinated us.

Near Elizabethtown, on the northern rim of the Pennyroyal, is Hodgenville, birthplace of Abraham Lincoln. The restored home of his parents is now a national historic shrine. Here people come to revere the man who stands head and shoulders above all other American leaders, looked upon by Europeans as the greatest statesman born on the North American continent.

I have often stood and wondered what might have happened if Lincoln's parents had not settled on this poor land. What if they had moved on another forty or fifty miles to the rich farmlands of the Kentucky counties on the Tennessee border? What difference might this have made in the destiny of Abraham Lincoln? He led the Union through the bloodiest war this country has ever fought, the Civil War or the War Between the States. Even now Kentuckians are divided over the proper name for this conflict, as they were divided in the war. Kentucky's motto was learned by hard and bitter experience: "United We Stand; Divided We Fall."

Only a few miles away, the better farmland of Todd County was the birthplace of Jefferson Davis, who led the Lost Cause of the Southern Confederacy. Todd County is plantation country, the area of the Pennyroyal akin to the Old South. And here, at the place of Davis's birth, a monument 351 feet tall has been erected. Built by his admirers in 1917–1924, it is the fourth tallest monument in the United States. Anyone passing by the site from sunrise to sunset will find a crowd of tourists. I have never driven past and found this shrine deserted.

I am the grandson of a Union soldier and a Confederate soldier. These men once lived two miles apart and never spoke to each other in their lives. I stop at the shrines commemorating the leaders of both the Union and the Confederacy.

The contrast between Abraham Lincoln and Jefferson Davis represents the contrasts that exist among the people of Kentucky and of the Pennyroyal. Each personified a distinctive way of life. Even the use of the English language differs within the Pennyroyal. In the northern area the people speak a dialect similar to that of the Western Coal Field. In the southern counties along the Tennessee border, the soft, slow English is like that of middle Tennessee or the Deep South. In the eastern panhandle the dialect is like that of the East Kentucky mountaineers.

Another Kentucky contrast is represented by the differences between the writing of Robert Penn Warren, a native of Guthrie, in Todd County, and my own writing. In his early novels, stories, and poems, Warren used subjects of this Old South region. I have done the same thing in my region. Yet how far apart we are, each writer in his own world, as different as Maine and California. People in the hills and mountains of East Kentucky would find it hard to understand people in the southern part of the Pennyroyal. The differences in the land have made the differences in our people. Warren's country is low, flat, fertile, inviting to farm; my country is high, rugged, ill-suited to farming. Warren's country includes the old slave-holding area, while mine knew only a few slaves, and with only a few exceptions all of these were freed long before the Civil War.

One of the greatest tourist attractions in Kentucky is the Land Between the Lakes, visited each year by thousands of vacationers. Kentucky Lake and Lake Barkley were created by dams built on the Tennessee and Cumberland rivers, and the area between was developed as a recreational area by the Tennessee Valley Authority. Kentucky's portion of the Land Between the Lakes was once a part of Trigg County, the most southwestern county in the Pennyroyal. This body of land (the upper two-thirds in Kentucky, the lower third in Tennessee) is from five to ten miles wide and forty miles from north to south. Its 170,000 acres of woodland make it a mecca for fishermen, campers, boaters, hunters, hikers, and swimmers. Environmental studies are also conducted here.

The area now has 5,000 deer of two species, white tail and fallow, the latter an Asian imported deer. There are from 400 to 500 wild turkeys, as well as rabbits, quail, raccoons, and bobcats. Fifty buffalo have been established. The area also supports 250 species of birds, including the bald eagle and the golden eagle.

One of the villages in this area before its development for recreation gave local, state, and federal authorities a lot of trouble. Golden Pond was a center for illegal whiskey production. The movie *The Moonshine War* was set in Golden Pond. I first heard of the town when I was in the hospital in Murray after my heart attack. Men were brought to the hospital each Saturday night to be treated for gunshot wounds or knife lacerations. I remember hearing eruptions among the antagonists, for the wounded from both sides came to the same hospital. Golden Pond's moonshine war is a thing of the past now. Those from all over America who visit Land Between the Lakes may never know what life was like here once, but they will enjoy the wildlife and the new recreational facilities.

This, then, is the Pennyroyal, the Pennyrile, a beautiful and historic part of my Kentucky.

MY WESTERN
COAL FIELD

THE WESTERN COAL FIELD is an unusual state in Kentucky: an area of high hills, some very high ones, too, tapering down into the rolling hills and flatlands of the Pennyroyal. The name Coal Field is inadequate to describe this distinctive area of ridges, rocks, and cliffs, with its man-made devastation. A more appropriate name would be Isolated Appalachia. I have called it Island of Integrity.

The 4,600 some square miles of this region are bordered on the north and west by the Ohio River, and on the south and east by the Pennyroyal. Remove Union County from those that comprise this district and you have an area the size of the country of Lebanon. But this state within Kentucky has slightly more than a quarter of a million people, while Lebanon has nearly four million.

I first visited this area in 1930 when I was a summer-school student at Peabody College in Nashville. I went home with Miss Georgene Crawford, a teacher, first cousin to "Happy" Chandler, later governor of Kentucky. She was the first to show me this region. I was twenty-three years old and from that time to the present I have often revisited this area. I found great similarities between the Western Coal Field and the East Kentucky mountains. I found sawbriars on the hill slopes. I found coal mines and old slate dumps, blue in the sunlight, with dark yawning mouths and dark mine props that always reminded me of dark teeth in an old man's gums. I also saw the white oaks, tough-butted, often used for mine props and ties for the tracks that ran back into the mines. People farmed poor slopes here, as people did in my East Kentucky mountains. All I saw here looked good to me on my first visit. Now this area attracts many tourists, as does the East Kentucky mountain region. Any Kentuckian from the eastern hills and mountains can feel at home here.

One thing that bothered me when I first visited the Western Coal Field was the speech. The pace was slower and the dialect was different in this area nearly three hundred miles southwest of where I lived. But the people of both Kentucky hill sections had more in common in life and living than the people of any other two sections of Kentucky. We had more in common than merely having seams of coal under our majestic hills.

This area remained antislavery and pro-Union during the Civil War. Although almost surrounded by proslavery people, the people of this little area had the integrity to stand alone. Their political faith has held strong, too. Until the unionization of the coal miners under Franklin D. Roosevelt, the mountain counties of East Kentucky had voted Republican since the time of the Civil War, but few now vote Republican regularly. In the Western Coal Field, in contrast, there are still Republican and near-Republican counties. They survive despite the pressures for poor people to change political parties to get jobs in a Democratic state. It is interesting that Kentucky has never had Republican control in both houses of the legislature and the governor's office at the same time. Yet, these people of the Coal Field have held to their Lincoln-Republican faith and have never changed. They are a strong-willed people.

The early settlers here were Methodists, and the Methodist circuit riders were influential in the area's early history. This rugged hill country didn't equal other sections of the state in rich farm and pasture land and the settlers tended to become isolated, much as they did in our eastern mountains. We too had Methodist circuit riders who went on horseback to preach, often to great crowds of people. They performed many a wedding ceremony, too, uniting a common-law man and wife. On occasion, when there had been no one available to marry them earlier, the couple's children listened to the ceremony of their parents' marriage. This was an "understood" marriage: a couple living together understood that they would be wed as soon as a preacher came to the neighborhood. The Methodist circuit riders also founded schools. Numbers of these schools grew and later flourished as colleges and universities.

Naomi and I drove through the Western Coal Field region with Dr. and Mrs. Ellis Ford Hartford. Dr. Hartford is an outstanding educator and author of books on education and philosophy. He was president and coordinator of the University of Kentucky's dozen centers of two- or three-year colleges in various parts of the state.

On this trip Dr. Hartford proudly showed us places in his region where old Methodist churches had once stood. A few remain today. When we arrived at one of these sites he proudly informed us, "My ancestors shouted all over this place. On both sides of my family I am descended from old Methodist circuit riders!"

Because Naomi's people, Norrises, Currys, Anglins, Kendalls, were the first to bring Methodism to southern Greenup County in about 1800, she and I found special pleasure in our rediscovery of this religious background.

What these early Methodist circuit riders were to pioneer Christianity and to the earliest, almost primitive efforts toward education, Dr. Hartford has been to the philosophy of education in his books. He himself is a product of the one-room school. Dr. Hartford's Isolated Appalachia, akin to my segment of Appalachia, was the last to let the one-room schools go.

Dr. and Mrs. Hartford drove us to Ohio County's seat, Hartford, population 596, named for his people. This is the county where he was born. It is very much like our other Appalachia, where the young people leave and not many "outsiders" move in. Only the older folk, descendants of pioneers, British Isles stock, mostly English, remain here.

I shall not forget this tour with the Hartfords. We stayed at Rough River Dam State Park. The Rough River flows through the heartland of the Western Coal Field and into the Green River, so called because its waters are always green except at floodtime. Eventually the Green River joins the Ohio. I wanted to follow the Rough River. So we did. I have always liked to follow rivers in Kentucky, or in other states, or even in foreign countries. I have liked to follow rivers large and small. Along the Rough River's banks are cliffs, jutted rocks, sandstone and limestone, cedars, pines, and occasional sycamores. It is one of the most scenic small rivers in Kentucky, in the United States. I wanted another night at Rough River Dam State Park, with its comfortable lodge and breakfasts of ham and eggs, grits, hashed brown potatoes, and hot biscuits.

As Ellis Hartford showed us his land, it seemed to be an island of integrity. Here was a native son, born and bred on this earth, who had been offered a high teaching position in Israel after the formation of that new country. Dr. Hartford was enthusiastic about that new land and its people and their progressive thought, but he did not go to Israel. He remained and worked with his own place and his own people. And that was the Western Coal Field of Kentucky.

I have spoken many times in the larger towns of this region. In Madisonville, for example, which is almost in the center and could well be called the capital of the region, I was accepted as I had never been accepted anywhere else. They knew me and my books better than I knew myself. Many remembered the contents of my books better than I did.

Fast-growing Owensboro is the largest city in this area. Here I have spoken many times. When Kentucky Wesleyan College moved from Winchester, Kentucky, it came to Owensboro. Here it has thrived and expanded to become one of the finest small, church-affiliated colleges in America. In addition to its good basketball team it has a fine literary magazine, *The Green River Review.*

On another occasion when I went to this area to speak in Henderson, I learned about one phase of entertainment in which we in East Kentucky are quite unlike the people of the Western Coal Field. Six miles from where I live there was once a racetrack. Prosperous Ashland, largest city in the East Kentucky mountains, was ten miles from the track. In Ashland, then as now, there was plenty of wealth. Many of the wealthy attended horse races in Lexington and at River Downs near Cincinnati, Ohio. But the people of this area didn't support Raceland Track and it failed. Church people in this area, almost all the denominations, rallied to oppose the racetrack. "Old Beelzebub's Sanctuary" they called it. Holiness preachers preached from their pulpits that Old Beelzebub rode jockey in every race. The sermons stirred up such animosity toward racing that our Raceland Track was a failure.

After I had spoken in Henderson, I was taken by educators from that city across a bridge over into a part of Kentucky on the other side of the Ohio River, near Evansville, Indiana. A change in the Ohio River's course had left this corner of Kentucky over there. It remains forever a little piece of Kentucky earth. And what had these Kentuckians of the Western Coal Field, these isolated Appalachians, done with that pocket of land? Two things. They had an excellent school over there. I spoke to the students of this school. And they had done something else. Horse racing was then illegal in the adjoining part of

Indiana. But this was Kentucky, really, in Indiana. They had established a racetrack for the Hoosiers and themselves which was a thriving concern. There was no failure here. Even with the broad Ohio separating this tiny speck of land from the mainland, it was still Kentucky!

There is another part of the Western Coal Field that I have seen annually for many years. Others have seen it, too, the millions of people driving through Ohio, Muhlenberg, and Hopkins counties on Western Kentucky Parkway. This is an area where the land comes down to waves of low hills. Under this land great deposits of coal have led to extensive stripmining. I believe this is where stripmining really began. At least, this is the place where it became colossal. It is difficult to believe that machines exist as large as those used to gouge out coal from this earth. Many people passing through are glad to drive on and do not stop. But I have stopped here to view what has been called reclamation of the disemboweled land.

My East Kentucky mountain region shares with the Western Coal Field the experience of victimization. Much of our earth has been destroyed. When I first viewed scenes of destruction along the Western Kentucky Parkway, I wrote of my feelings in a poem. I named it "Hell."

Even before stripmining in the Western Kentucky Coal Field, this area had been referred to as the "badlands" of Kentucky. Its poor, rocky soil, low hills of sassafras, sawbriars, scrub oaks and pines, which resembled portions of my East Kentucky mountains, were areas ill-suited to farming. There were narrow valleys with bottomland which had some good farmland. But the wealth of this land was what lay under it, coal. It could have been called a "golden land" until its coal was stripmined. And the vegetation that covered it was beautiful to see compared with the stripmined areas.

Here the guts of the earth are upturned into nonproductive soil. Here shale and slate are piled up high and lack sufficient fertility to grow a plant or feed a bird. In a pitiful gesture of reclamation, a few scraggly pines cling tenaciously to soil that cannot feed them. Most of the planted seedlings have died. The effort at reclaiming this soil has been in vain. Can it ever be made productive again? Better to leave it as a tourist attraction for decades to come. It is wasteland. The despoilers have written their message on our land. They have reached a pinnacle of destruction of our Kentucky earth.

Someday, perhaps, busloads of tourists will come to visit this area of the state. It will be called the Bad Lands of Kentucky. I have visited South Dakota with its natural Bad Lands. Kentucky's will be man-made Bad Lands. That desolate and dramatic pocket of South Dakota has but little growth or vegetation. Nevertheless it has more than the Bad Lands of western Kentucky have now or will have.

As a tourist attraction, Kentucky's Bad Lands may pay off in the future. This will be a way to make this robbed and desecrated land pay. It hasn't any farming value; how can it be taxed by county and commonwealth? As an attraction it could produce revenue and tax. This is land, Kentucky land, and land is precious over the world. It grows more precious as the world's populations expand.

The people of this region have a sense of humor. They not only repeat jokes but they make up jokes. Among the coal miners and coal strippers of the Western Coal Field this is particularly true, even more than in my own region. In my mountains, bloody clan wars and struggles surrounding the unionization of coal mines have combined with old Scottish ballads of war and death to create a special kind of stories and music. Our humor has not been like the humor of the Ozark Mountains or that of our brothers and sisters in the Western Coal Field.

In this stripmine area of Kentucky, a wry kind of humor has originated. An example is a proposal for use of the black water that comes from the stripmining and gives off an unpleasant smell. There is talk of bottling this blackish water and selling it as Black Diamond perfume. And it is said that this stagnant water breeds a different kind of mosquito, one large enough to fly down and carry away a woman's purse. A bite from one of these extraordinary mosquitoes can kill a man, a cow, a horse, or a swine, or even a tree. Of course, neither humans nor animals can drink such water. When you drive through this area, stop to see the vegetation it has killed. Nothing fed by this water will grow. So it is a bitter humor, indeed.

In these Bad Lands of Kentucky the fabulous mosquito may become as legendary in years to come as Hodag, an animal that fed on bulldogs before breakfast, about which we once heard in the lumberjack country of Rhinelander, Wisconsin. Tales of the man-made Bad Lands may help call attention to the greatest human destruction of earth anywhere in Kentucky.

It is interesting that coal miners in Kentucky's Western Coal Field have fewer strikes than those in any area where coal is mined in this nation. They have a character all their own, different from all others, except perhaps that of the East Kentucky mountains. An island unto itself is my Isolated Appalachia.

MY JACKSON PURCHASE

LET'S TALK ABOUT another world of Kentucky, a world in contrast to the East Kentucky mountains. A crow flying from eastern Pike County across mountains, rivers, hills, and flatlands would cover 400 miles before reaching Hickman, in Fulton County, near the mighty Mississippi. The Pike County mountaineer lives in a deep valley bordered by high mountains which allow the sun to shine on his valley less than half the day, and he is probably a coal miner who raises a garden and "truck patches" on land almost too steep to stand on. His fellow Kentuckian over in Fulton County raises cotton, corn, and soybeans on land as level as a floor and comparable in fertility to the Nile Valley in Egypt.

What do you think these men have in common who seem so different, who have grown up in such separate worlds? The Pike County native, if he's descended from pioneers, probably had ancestors who fought in the Union army to free slaves. The Fulton County man, if a descendant of pioneers, probably had ancestors who fought in the Confederate army. One knows the black gold from the coal mines. He knows the narrow-gauged valleys and has to look up to see the sun. He does not have enough land to be a big-time farmer; his acreage may contain scarcely enough level land for a garden. Many in the coal mine camps have truck patches only large enough for beans, potatoes, and corn for the table. The Fulton County farmer has room in plenty for garden and truck farming. He works his fields by riding farm machinery from sunrise to sunset. He can see for miles in all directions across as fine a farmland as ever the crow flew over.

The Fulton County farmer lives in one of the eight counties in the Jackson Purchase. The Pike County coal miner lives in the largest county in square miles in all Kentucky. But people cannot live on most of those square miles for it is difficult to find a lot level enough to build a house on. I priced land once in Floyd County, which adjoins Pike, and I couldn't believe the asking price: forty thousand dollars for one level acre. There are few places in Pike and Floyd counties to build houses and improve yards and gardens. A farmer from Fulton County could not believe this unless he had visited the East Kentucky mountain counties. Ten years ago, at the time I priced the land in Floyd, forty thousand dollars would have purchased 120 acres of fine farmland in the Jackson Purchase. Now, with the inflation of our dollar and the deflation of real value, the price of farmland in the Purchase has shot skyward. Farmers from many places are wanting to "buy it up."

The Jackson Purchase is on the point of the Kentucky plowshare, surrounded on the north by the Ohio River, on the east by Kentucky Lake (the impoundment of the Tennessee River) and Lake Barkley (the impoundment of the Cumberland River), on the west by the mighty Mississippi, and on the south by the Tennessee state line. The Purchase is the northern tip of the level Mississippi Embayment extending up from the south. It is an area of approximately 2,400 square miles, a little larger than Delaware, with some 168,000 people.

The early pioneers of the Jackson Purchase were never a landlocked people, as were those in the East Kentucky mountains or in sections of the Pennyroyal. They could always travel by boat, taking advantage of the three rivers on their borders. Kentucky and Barkley dams now create bodies of water large enough for ships. These people remain original in customs and way of life, different from the people of any other section of the state. They are lowlanders; the East Kentucky mountaineers are the highlanders. In Scotland, living in the Lowlands or the Highlands makes a lot of difference. Scotland is two countries. Much the same is true with the Jackson Purchase and the East Kentucky mountains.

I visited the Purchase later than any other area of Kentucky. I went there to speak at Murray State College (now a university) and I have returned many times. Before I went there, the Purchase seemed to be on the other side of the world to a hill man from the northeast corner of Kentucky. I was closer to Pittsburgh, Columbus, or Chicago than to the Purchase. I had traveled to these places for speeches, and by preference, before I went to the Purchase.

Now, speaking at Murray, I discovered another state within my state. I had not found any Kentuckians exactly like these people. One excellent educator in the region asked me to run for governor. He knew I was a Republican and would have little chance for winning, but he liked my ideas on teaching and education. He said, "We can pull the First District for you." The First District must be a hundred to one Democratic! Of course, I wouldn't have run for governor under any consideration, but nowhere in Kentucky had I been paid a finer compliment.

On a later visit to Murray, to speak to the teachers of the First Educational District, I had my first heart attack, a massive coronary. I survived because of that extra ounce of stamina, that W-Hollow endurance; but I lay in the Murray Hospital for seven days before even having my clothes removed, and forty-eight days before I could go home. I was in bed approximately eleven months.

I believe that if I had not been at Murray, in the Jackson Purchase, when I had my heart attack, I wouldn't be alive today. My wife Naomi and our daughter Jane came to live there while I was in the hospital. Jane entered school there for two months. I will never forget what the people did for us. And what they did for us they did for others. One family from Michigan had a car wreck there. The people of Murray kept the family until the father was able to go home. They are of old American stock, down-to-earth people with generous hearts. That was when I fell in love with the Jackson Purchase people.

Recovery from my heart attack required almost two years. Since then I have returned to the Purchase to speak many times in the larger cities—Paducah, Mayfield, Benton, and back to Murray—and in some of the county school systems. Finally, I spent five summers teaching at a creative writing workshop at Murray State. Naomi and I became friends with people in all corners of the Jackson Purchase. I got to know hundreds of students from all the counties in this area: what they thought, what they ate for breakfast, what dreams they cherished. If I had been a younger man I would have purchased a few hundred acres of their farmland, although I lived hundreds of miles away. The distance, when we first started driving to Murray, following a direct line from northeast Kentucky to southwest Kentucky, was 508 miles. It was a hard day's driving. Now, with improved roads, it is approximately 400 miles.

Our five summers at Murray State University were happy days. A teacher of poetry, Lee Boyce Pennington, one of my former students, and his wife Joy, a young and eager couple, usually accompanied us in our drives over the Purchase. How many times? Maybe the Penningtons kept a record. We didn't. Lee Pennington is from the high and rugged hills of western Greenup County.

As we drove over the Purchase we had a little game. We knew that the First District was solidly Democratic in its politics and so we tried to find an unpaved county road in all of the Jackson Purchase. If I remember correctly we found a few. But almost all the roads were paved, quite a contrast to East Kentucky. Roads were so easy to build here, and so difficult to construct in our own mountainous area.

When we traveled we were puzzled by some of the buildings we found on farms: low, cone-shaped structures with small chimneys. We later learned that these were tobacco barns where farmers cured the "dark-fired" tobacco used for cigars and chewing tobacco. It is not like the white burley grown in most of the rest of Kentucky, fine cigarette tobacco so thin one can almost read a newspaper through the leaf. Even in its tobacco, the Jackson Purchase is different.

Robert Penn Warren based his first novel, *Night Rider*, on the tobacco growers' war in the Jackson Purchase. My teacher at Lincoln Memorial University, Harry Harrison Kroll, also wrote about this dramatic tobacco war of 1906–1908 in a nonfiction book titled *Riders in the Night*. Both accounts told of the struggle among the people of the Purchase who grew dark-fired tobacco and sold it to powerful monopolies.

With Lee and Joy Pennington as our traveling companions, we covered all of the Purchase. One Sunday we drove to Fulton County to see a part we had missed. We had to drive down into Tennessee and come back up on a road into Kentucky's westernmost possession, a piece of land cut away from the rest of the state by a bend in the Mississippi River. The area is not large. It would make one extensive farm. When Lee and I looked out over this fertile land, each of us wished that our fathers could have had such land when they were farming back in East Kentucky's high hills. People on this fine flat land could not have imagined our uptilted farms.

Plant almost anything in the Purchase and it will grow. One tree I remember was said to be the largest tree ever seen to grow in Kentucky. This land reminds me of the

Nile Valley in Egypt, the finest farmland in the world. When I taught at American University in Cairo, the soil along the Nile fascinated me. It was unbelievably productive and grew two crops each year. The topsoil went down ninety-two feet and Egyptian farmers' hands had fondled and caressed it for five thousand years. If it were not for the Nile and its delta, the Egyptians would starve. I can think of no area in the world to compare to this Jackson Purchase farmland except the fertile Nile Valley and its delta. Maybe the topsoil here doesn't go down ninety-two feet; I don't know how many feet it goes down. And the soil here isn't alluvium, as that of the Nile Valley is. But this area is equal to the finest farmlands in the world. I doubt if many people of the Jackson Purchase realize the similarity of their land to that of the Nile. They take their soil and its fertility for granted.

Another Sunday we visited Hickman. When I drive from Murray over to Hickman I am always looking for palm trees. I know this is too far north for palms to grow. But the landscape makes me think of Egypt and of palms.

At Hickman we stood and watched the rolling waters of the broad Mississippi River. One of my students from Hickman had written an excellent story on this river. So I had to go and see the Mississippi rolling along. Here I had a mishap. After viewing the river for hours, we went back to the car. As I was pulling the car door shut behind me it caught my ear. Except for my heart attack, I have never had more pain. I never knew before that pain of the ear is next to pain in the eye. The car door cut a hole through my ear. A passerby happened along who knew me through my books, and directed us to a hospital in Union City, Tennessee, where emergency patients were accepted on Sunday. Nine stitches were taken in my ear to close the hole. I will never forget the young man who directed us to this hospital. He exemplified the best of the Jackson Purchase people. They are hospitable and friendly people and never shy from strangers.

But there are dangers in this country. Where the land is level as a floor, tornadoes sometimes come in summer and pull soybeans up from the earth by the roots, turn over houses and barns, and leave paths of devastation. I have seen fields of dark green corn, as fine as any in America, flattened by tornadoes. Could a man in Pike County, in the mountains of East Kentucky, imagine this? I doubt that he could, with his mountains to protect him. How could a tornado hit his deep, protected valleys?

Drive over this area in the growing season, as I have, and see fields of cotton, hemp, strawberries, sweet potatoes, corn, soybeans, oats, barley, wheat, okra, sugar corn, and popcorn. See cattle farms and dairy herds. Above all, see the dark-fired tobacco growing higher than a man's head, set in motion by the continuous wind over this flat land.

Residents of this area often feel they are "stepchildren of Kentucky." But the natives here would never trade the name Kentucky, which holds together all of its different states within a state, to be a part of any bordering state.

The people here have great kinship with the people in Arkansas and Missouri, just across the Mississippi, even in their excellent cooking. Black-eyed peas and catfish are two of my favorite foods in the Purchase. Their streams, rivers, and lakes abound in catfish, and they grow plenty of black-eyed peas.

People here have kinship with west Tennesseeans and northern Mississippians, too. Paducah has a television station which covers this area. But they also get TV reception from Nashville, Tennessee. The Paducah *Sun Democrat* competes for circulation with the *Nashville Banner* and *Tennessean,* and the Memphis *Commercial Appeal.* Memphis, two slow hours away, is like a capital city to people in the Purchase. Here is where they go for much of their shopping, entertainment, and visits to friends. This is the large city closest to them and they love it. They don't go north and they don't go east. They go to Memphis.

After reading a great deal about bussing, I once had a crazy idea while teaching at Murray: wouldn't it be wonderful if people from this area could be bussed across Kentucky to our region? Then people from my East Kentucky, many of whom have never seen cotton grow, could be bussed to see the Jackson Purchase. Thus Kentuckians from the extreme ends of this commonwealth could get to know one another.

Actually, we are strangers to one another. Black-eyed peas, for instance, aren't considered an important food in my Kentucky mountains; they are considered feed for cattle. Gradually, however, people are beginning to realize what they've missed these many years. There are other foods, okra and peanuts for example, that are special to the Purchase. Many youth in the Kentucky mountain area have never seen these grow. This massive bussing wouldn't be a bad idea for the people who live at opposite ends of Kentucky, but it has never been given a trial.

With all my speaking and teaching in the Purchase, and with my heart attack and long recuperative period in the hospital at Murray, the kindness of the people of the Purchase endeared them to me and my family. Aside from my hill and mountain area, the Bluegrass, and Louisville, I know this area of Kentucky, this extremity of the state, best.

So, feeling the way I did about the Jackson Purchase people after we really became acquainted, I wanted to do something for them in return. I had received requests from Syracuse University, Yale University, and the Library of Congress for manuscripts of some of my books or poems or stories. But I had a different idea. I didn't want them scattered here and there. They had to be in one body, one deposit, and this would require not a shelf, not a box, not a room, but many rooms. I didn't want them to leave the state. And I didn't want them at one of our good institutions of higher learning near my home for a very definite reason. People from my area might examine some of these manuscripts too carefully, hunting for characterizations of people they knew. They would find them, too. A good 400 miles from home there wouldn't be many of the merely curious who would drive to search the manuscripts. Murray State University, I reasoned, was the logical place to deposit my manuscripts.

So it was agreed with Dr. Marvin Wrather that my manuscripts, scrapbooks, copies of early books, and other items associated with my writing would go to Murray State University on long-time loan. They prepared one room, but it would not hold all the material. Then they prepared three rooms. They may have to expand even more when all the material is finally gathered. I presented Murray State University, the chief institution of higher learning in the Jackson Purchase, with as fine a bouquet as I could to show my appreciation and my love of this area and its people.

MY LOUISVILLE: CITY STATE

KENTUCKY has been divided by geologists and historians into six states, and one of these, the Pennyroyal, can be divided into three smaller parts. But I have to add a seventh section, which can be likened to a city state in ancient Greece. This is Louisville and Jefferson County, where over one-fifth of all of Kentucky's population is concentrated. On a mere 375 square miles live over 700,000 people.

Louisville is Kentucky's largest city, but not all Kentucky roads lead to Louisville, as all roads lead to Chicago, or Atlanta, or Columbus, Ohio, cities that are dominant in their states (two are capitals) and approximately midway in geography. All roads lead to certain large foreign cities, too: London, Paris, Rome, Cairo, Stockholm. But not all roads lead to our Louisville.

Louisville is a city different from all others in Kentucky, a city not attached to any other in ways and customs. Louisville is Louisville and has been from its beginning. It is not central Kentucky. It is not a city in one of the states within this commonwealth. It is a section unto itself with a small land area, definitely one country, a populated area with the Ohio River for its northern and western boundaries.

We in the East Kentucky mountains have our Paintsville, Pikeville, Prestonsburg, London, Middlesboro, Ashland (our largest and dominant city), all flavored by life in and of the region. We have our roads leading to Ashland. In the Bluegrass all roads certainly lead to Lexington. Then there are other Bluegrass cities and towns: Winchester, Richmond, Danville, Mount Sterling, Versailles, Paris, and Bardstown. The Pennyroyal, in its variations of landscapes and people, has for its capital Bowling Green, once the capital of Kentucky under the Confederacy. It has such different places as Hodgenville, Elizabethtown, Hopkinsville, Somerset, Glasgow, all cities attached to their particular areas. At the heart of the Western Coal Field is Madisonville; Owensboro is its northern capital. The Jackson Purchase has its Paducah, Murray, Mayfield, Hickman, and Benton, cities indigenous to the area, all flavored with the atmosphere of the Old South. They really belong to this very different state within Kentucky.

Louisville is different from all these other cities and towns attached to their separate regions. Louisville stands alone like an ancient city state. Jefferson County still has farming and grazing areas. It also has Middletown, Shively, Valley Station, and Jeffersontown. But people living in these towns can see Louisville spreading toward them.

I am not a city man. I love land, to the ends of the world. And I especially love my land: Kentucky and the United States of America. I have lived in cities. Now I visit them only when I have to. But my love for Louisville began when I first visited there in 1923. I rode a troop train through and then returned a few times from Fort Knox.

During the Depression years, even on my small teaching salary of $100 a month, I never missed a Kentucky Education Association meeting. These were always held in Louisville. I attended these gatherings each year I taught or was in an administrative position in a Kentucky school.

Louisville was the first large city I ever saw. After the publication of *Man with a Bull-Tongue Plow* in 1934, I was invited to Louisville for a number of talks. One was to an English Department group at the University of Louisville. This time I went in a bit of triumph. Heretofore, when I went as a teacher or school administrator, I stayed at the old Chesterton House for two dollars a night. But on this trip, as author of a big book of poetry which was getting good reviews, I stayed in style at an uptown hotel, one of Louisville's best, the Brown. If Louisville had accepted me, I had certainly accepted Louisville and have ever since. It is a city that has always been good to me. I hoped Louisvillians would never read a poem I wrote and published in an Eastern magazine, called "The Cities." Its first line said, "All cities are a little piece of hell."

Louisville, since I became acquainted there, has never been without its circle of prose writers and poets. On this first journey of triumph to Louisville I met Cale Young Rice. I had heard all kinds of rumors about this poet, husband to Alice Hegan Rice, who wrote *Mrs. Wiggs of the Cabbage Patch.* I heard that Cale Young Rice, when dining with a woman, might reach under the table and pull off her slipper. When I met him, I was surprised to discover the best-dressed writer I had ever seen at that time or since. Immaculately groomed, he was better dressed than Lord Astor of England, at whose residence in London I later stayed. Rice was as fresh as a wind blown from over a Jefferson County wheat field. Actually the man was wearing the first spats I had ever seen. His conversation was literary, excellent. I was hungry for what he had to say. Our poetry was different. Different geographic regions in Kentucky had produced two literary strangers.

I met Barbara and Dwight Anderson. Dwight was the head of the Music Department at the University of Louisville. He tested my taste for music on the piano. I heard for the first time "Clair de Lune." I asked for Schubert's "Serenade." The fact that I was from the East Kentucky mountains and liked classical music surprised him. His wife Barbara had written and published a good novel. This was the beginning of a long friendship.

It was through the Andersons that I met Elizabeth Madox Roberts. I was deeply impressed with her. She told me how to write a novel; she was a teacher herself. She said that I should let the main ridge in my hill country be the main character, and the spur ridges, those attached to the main ridge, be my minor characters. She couldn't have stated it better to me in a few words. Nowhere in Kentucky outside of Louisville could I have met a group such as this.

Louisville, I learned, was something more than I had found it to be when I first went there wearing an ill-fitting khaki uniform, leggings, and brogan shoes. It was more than I had thought when I attended the Kentucky Education Association meetings there once a year. Louisville had three types of educational institutions: public, private, and parochial. There were good music recitals and plays in Louisville. I have never seen a public library that equaled Louisville's. There was culture in Louisville. When I received my first introductions, I had never been exposed to these aspects of culture. It happened first in Louisville. Louisville was a different part of Kentucky. I recognized it then when I was very young. I know it now that I am a much older man.

Even the language was a little different from my own, I found. Being from the Kentucky mountains, I could have dismissed this as "city talk," or "proper talk," as we used to say. But I would have been wrong. I wasn't the first to discover this. A graduate student at the University of Louisville who had a keen ear for languages and dialects did a master of arts thesis comparing the dialect of Louisvillians with the dialect spoken in Ohio, Indiana, and

Illinois. She concluded that the language spoken by Louisville people was a midwestern dialect.

Louisville has a newspaper that is rated third in the nation: *The Courier-Journal.* For sheer excellence of writing I don't know a newspaper in the United States, including the *New York Times,* that is better. I would have to go to England and read the London *Observer* or the Manchester *Guardian* to find one as good. I can pick up a London *Observer* in Africa and even if it is a year old and all the news surrounding a certain issue is dead, I can still read the paper for the beauty of its style. *The Courier-Journal* is much the same. I don't always agree with its editorials. I think many are biased. Then I look in the thinking mirror at myself and wonder if the editorials are biased or if I am biased!

My Louisville is an original area, surrounded by land that is forever Kentucky, where an acre sells for ten to twenty thousand dollars and more; a land that has produced, among other things, giants in journalism.

Where is there another city that names its public elementary and secondary schools for teachers and writers? One of the living monuments was named for Robert Frost. The Jesse Stuart High School was named for me. I have a living monument. Since I knew Robert Frost, I think about the future relationships of our schools in Louisville. When we are both gone, our schools will still be close together.

There is not another city in the United States where so many books of poetry are sold in proportion to the population. No wonder poets in Kentucky and over the United States can think of Louisville as the "poet's city." Although this might not advertise it well in America, there is one city I know in the world where such a title would be welcome. It is Shiraz in Iran, where massive tombs are erected not to political leaders but to poets. Sadi and Hafiz, Persian poets, have great tombs erected to them in this land of poets and poetry lovers.

From the early days of the Great Depression to the present, I have been asked to autograph books in Louisville. I began with *Man with a Bull-Tongue Plow*. It was poetry, and times were hard, and I signed only a few copies. Since then I have signed as many as a thousand copies of a book in one day. This happened with my novel *Taps for Private Tussie*. I signed seven hundred copies on another occasion; always in the hundreds. Louisville is a fine city for the writer, the book lover. Have I known another city in any other country that is comparable? If so, it is Edinburgh, Scotland, famed as the cultural city of that land and one of the most cultural in all of Europe.

As it has been in the past, so in the present an urge compels me to return to certain landscapes in my region, my state, my country, my world. I grow hungry to see again a crown colony and four countries from the Middle East to the Orient. So, too, I am compelled to return to Louisville. Cities do not usually appeal to me. But Louisville is different. It is a city state unto itself. It is a unique part of Kentucky. It is my Louisville.

MY U.S.A.

ALTHOUGH I WAS BORN and lived in the United States for twenty-nine years, I never knew it until I was fortunate enough to receive a Guggenheim Fellowship and spend fourteen months in Scotland and traveling throughout Europe. After visiting twenty-eight countries in Europe, I knew the United States as I had never known it before.

In all my teaching I have recommended travel to youth. I recommend it to middle-aged and older people if they have not traveled. Travel is education. When Naomi and I spent a year in Egypt teaching, we spent Christmas and vacation days, and even long weekends, traveling with our daughter Jane to other countries. We often flew up to Beirut, Lebanon. We visited Saudi Arabia, Jordan, Syria, and the Holy Land. When the school year was over we spent most of the summer visiting European countries that had been part of the Roman Empire.

After we returned home that autumn, I was asked to speak at Ohio University and while there to watch a homecoming football game. I'd not seen a good football game in over two years, and I was hungry to see one. I sat in a special box seat, but this time, as much as I loved football, I never saw the game. Instead I saw the American flag in a stiff breeze out before me. I realized what the symbol of our country, the American flag, really meant to me. I sat there watching the flag with a fountain pen in my pocket but not any paper. I wrote a mental story, an article, an essay, or a speech that only at that time I could have written. I did it then. I tried to do it later, to put it on paper, but I couldn't.

Since that time I've returned to countries I had visited, and I've traveled in many more. I've traveled in ninety countries altogether, some only once, some as many as sixteen times. Now I feel definitely that I know what my United States is. Again, I have said many times on the platform when I have been questioned about the United States, "If you have traveled and have found a greater country than the United States, tell me where it is, and I'll cancel everything I'm doing and be there in a week!"

No one has ever answered that challenge. The United States is greater than any country I have visited. People in other countries who can express themselves freely know this, too. I don't know how many people, young and old, have begged me, actually cried for me, to get them to America. On several occasions when I was speaking and I said kind words for the country I was in, I'd be interrupted by people who would shout, "I'll trade places with you."

Certainly we make mistakes in America. And we'll go on making mistakes. Certainly we have problems in America. We've had so many I wouldn't know what to do without them. We'll go on having problems in the United States. No country in the world is "problem free." And when the United States was criticized by audiences in a question and answer period after a lecture, I used to say, "Be careful what you say! Your people from this country helped do that. The United States has people from every country in the world."

The United States is a people's dream. We live better, have better food, better schools, better roads, more vehicles, more merchandise for sale in our stores than any country I have ever been in. We have more and better farming, the greatest farming in the world. No country has better trained school teachers and better schools, from kindergarten to the graduate level. Too many Americans don't realize what America means to them and to the world.

I have traveled all over America, as well as around the world. In many of these states, I have looked at the land with a covetous eye. I could settle happily in almost any state, but I'd want to choose my spot.

In Maine, for instance, with its rockbound coast, where I first visited in 1935, I could live happily somewhere in the country near Portland, in sight and sound of the Atlantic. Or I'd like to live on a farm in the northern part of Vermont or New Hampshire, where a barn is connected to the house by a hallway. What beautiful northern country! In Massachusetts, Connecticut, Rhode Island, I'd like to live on a small farm if I could find one where I could see and hear the Atlantic. The inland New England states have some beautiful countryside and small towns and villages which would be nice places to live in. I like the cleanliness of this area, unequaled anywhere in the United States except Wisconsin. New England is so much like England, Wales, Ireland, and Scotland.

In New York, I'd certainly take upstate, preferably in or close to the Finger Lakes area or the Adirondack Mountains. In Pennsylvania it would be the Pocono Mountains. What autumn beauty! In Maryland it would have to be around Frostburg. New Jersey is two states, north and south. I'd choose a small farm, if I could find one, up the coast from Atlantic City. In Delaware, I'd like a farm overlooking Delaware Bay.

In Virginia, I'd choose Lee County, the Powell Valley, land where my ancestors lived. In North Carolina, I'd choose a green deep valley in the Great Smokies. In South Carolina, I would choose anywhere, but preferably in or close to Columbia. In Georgia, definitely at West

Point or Brunswick. In Alabama, not in but near Mobile in a small village on that beautiful Gulf Coast. This goes for Mississippi, too, somewhere near Biloxi on a small plantation where I could be near the white sands along the Gulf of Mexico. I would, also, like a plantation in that fertile Mississippi soil north of Vicksburg and west of Winona.

In Florida, if I chose to live there, it would be in the Tampa area, or at Boca Raton, or at Fort Myers, the most beautiful city in the state. Florida is a state I've visited many times, for our only child, her husband, and our two grandsons now are permanent citizens of Florida. But it's not a state where I would choose to live. I prefer a region where we can know the changes of the four seasons, the coloring of leaves in autumn.

In Tennessee, I'd choose to live in that beautiful limestone valley near Greeneville. All of Tennessee, a state I know so well, is a nice place to live. In West Virginia, also neighbor to my Kentucky, I'd choose near Wheeling, or a farm on the Ohio River near Point Pleasant. In Ohio, I'd pick a farm in that great farming country between Washington Court House and Dayton.

All of Indiana is a special state for me, with its farmlands, writers, and songs. So many times I've traveled over it. But I'd prefer a big farm with plenty of sycamores where I could raise corn and soybeans. To live in Illinois, I would choose a farm up in that fine farmland near Rockford. I also like the area around Bloomington, a beautiful city where I once stayed a while after a speaking engagement and finished a junior book I was writing.

In earlier years I traveled in every county in Michigan. Ionia in the lower peninsula is as pretty a small town as I've ever seen. Around Ionia or up at Marquette on Lake Superior in the upper peninsula are places I'd choose to own property and live. For my work in the upper peninsula I was later given an honorary degree by Northern Michigan University in Marquette.

In Wisconsin I could live most anywhere. The people make Wisconsin. It's a state I've learned to love, a great farm and dairy state, and the cleanest state in America. If I were to pick a city, I'd pick Madison, of course, but there is a northern area in this northern state, around Rhinelander, south of Michigan's upper peninsula. Up here it is July, August, and winter, and the only tires sold are snow tires. The people are mostly of Scandinavian descent, plus many American Indians. If I were younger, I could easily live here and relish the hard winters.

In Minnesota I know it would be rough, but I'd choose up around Bemidji, in the northern part of the state, near where the Mississippi River begins at Itasca. I'd like just to live in that small town with Swedes, Norwegians, and Finns, up among the American Vikings. I especially like the food up there. I'd have July and August for summer and the rest of the year for winter. But when the leaves turned on the maples, I'd like to fly twice daily, as long as the autumn season lasted, down to Saint Paul and back to Bemidji just to see below me multicolored clouds of leaves dotted with blue lakes.

Iowa is a great state, with its rich farm earth that produces great harvests, its clean cities, and good schools. I could live many places there. But I'd prefer O'Brien County, out somewhere near Primghar in that wonderful farm and cattle country. When I worked here with teachers, I visited farms. I loved this area. Or I'd take somewhere in the Ozark Mountains in Missouri, or around Little Rock, which is a beautiful city, in Arkansas.

In Louisiana my choice has to be in the country outside of Ruston. I've traveled and worked all over this state (two states really, one in the north and one in the south), but I've been in Ruston so many times it seems like home to return.

In the empire of Texas, a country within a country, there are several places I like: the Panhandle up around Amarillo, or Waco and the Brazos River, or Laredo, or

Dallas. I like Texas. But I'd settle for a cattle ranch and some open space somewhere near Waco. I like the spirit of Texans!

I'd like to live in western Oklahoma in the plains area, where as far as the eye can see is land, land and sky. Here is music of wind and loneliness. Then there is Kansas, one of the flat states in America, and one of the finest farm states, where the surface of the land turns golden when the wheat ripens. Somehow, I much prefer western Kansas and the Great Plains area. I would choose Hayes or Winfield or one of the areas that surround them. But my preference would be one of the great ranches where they measure by square miles instead of acres; where, if they must have a fence, they use stone posts from which to string wires. To see a tree here is a welcome sight on these vast plains where the winds play symphonies. Out here there is a different kind of meadowlark, one I've never seen elsewhere, which sings lyrical songs. What greatness and vastness here, where man knows he is a being and can never lose his identity.

In Nebraska, I would choose to live near Nebraska State University in Lincoln, not in the city but on a nearby farm. Around Grand Island is a beautiful farm area, too. Then I'd like living on "the bluffs" near Omaha, looking down on the Mississippi River. The Indians preferred this, too.

Why people continually leave the Dakotas I do not understand. People have continually left my East Kentucky mountains since World War II, but not because they wanted to; they left the land they loved for economic reasons. But the Dakotas have some of the best farmland in the world. As a younger man, despite the long hard winters, I could have lived in and loved either state.

In North Dakota I would have chosen a wheat farm of 50,000 acres north of Grand Forks. Up there the tumbleweeds grow so big North Dakotans have found a use for this useless weed. They use them for Christmas trees. While up there working once I wrote a story called "Tale of the Tumbleweed." It is one of my unpublished manuscripts.

South Dakota in summer is one of the beautiful states of America. It has been classified as our most rural state, with Mississippi second, and Kentucky third. Here is some of the finest, most productive soil on earth. I've visited farms here, looked over crops and cattle, and envied farmers with their great grain harvests. I've worked all over this state. To live here I would prefer a farm in western South Dakota not too far from Rapid City, near South Dakota's Bad Lands.

In Montana, a sparsely settled big state where I've traveled as tourist and speaker, I'd choose to live in the green contours of hills against blue skies near Jackson and the Continental Divide. Here short wheat is grown. Land greens up in spring and summer and the clear trout streams cascade down slopes undefiled, flashing bright in the sunlight, like wind-rustled silver ribbons against a green background. It's beautiful country. I like Billings, too, in south central Montana.

In Wyoming, where I once drove 123 miles and counted three ranch houses, I'd prefer to live in the north, around Sheridan. In Colorado, I'd like a farm east of Denver, in sight of the snow-capped Rockies. But if I had to live in a city I'd prefer Boulder and its nearby scenic Rocky Mountain National Park. In New Mexico, a state I know less than many others, I'd prefer to live in the farm area near Albuquerque. I know the spot, near a slope filled with pines. I can still see it in a mental picture.

Arizona is a state where it isn't hard for me to decide. Here I've worked and traveled many times, first in 1940 as a tourist. I'd choose Phoenix first. Here is one of the unique cities of America, with fast-building suburban areas now becoming cities. It's a city in which to live and work or retire. Much of the Arizona desert looks inviting to me, too. Even the pack rat on the desert there is different from the one found in my East Kentucky mountains.

In Utah, where I went early as a tourist and later many times to speak, I was offered positions, inviting ones, in their colleges and a university. I had so much in common with their Mormons, although I was not a Mormon. In my youth my family had known struggles like those of the Mormons, who came to a new land with a dream, almost a wasteland, which they made blossom. I have never worked among people more frugal (they have had to be) or with greater integrity. I could have lived anywhere among the Mormons. But of all Utah, the one place I would choose to live, on a farm, of course, would be close to Logan. Here is one of those magnificent spots where nature has made mountains, passes through the mountains, and blue skies beyond, with white clouds floating high above all. Here, in this cattle, sheep, and farming country, are green valleys, meadows, clean tended crops of corn, beans, potatoes, hay. Here are gardens extraordinary, a university, and Logan, with clean, wide streets and shops enough to fill the city dwellers' and farmers' needs. Here is an ideal small city in one of the most fantastically beautiful places on earth. And here are the Mormons, more or less all in one body, while we in Kentucky are of seven sections, different and divided in all respects but with one state flag and one name holding us together.

I've traveled through Idaho twice from the Canadian border to the south, but I've never worked in Idaho. It's one of the five states where I haven't. I cannot make a fair conclusion, but the place where I'd choose to own land and live would be the sloping lands along the Bitterroot Mountains.

In the state of Washington, I would choose the farm area in and around Tacoma. This is certainly an attractive area in a state where I have traveled twice as a tourist but where I have never worked, due, on two occasions, to great snowfalls when my bookings had to be cancelled. But in Oregon my mind was made up in my several visits. If I were to be a permanent resident of this state, I would choose, and very quickly, a farm outside and very near to Portland.

In Nevada, a state where I've spoken, and where I have taught at the University of Nevada in Reno, I would have only one choice, Reno. Here the Truckee River, with the finest irrigated garden land in the world in its valley, rises in Lake Tahoe and sinks in Pyramid Lake. This is a state where virtually all rivers sink. Naomi, Jane, then sixteen, and I lived in and loved Reno, a city that had more than gambling. If I were to live there, I wouldn't be a farmer but a teacher and writer.

I went to California at an early age and worked across the state; I returned twice later to work, and have gone back for single appearances on other occasions. Three times I was offered a teaching position at the University of California at Berkeley, a very inviting one in 1940, when I was thirty-three. I loved California then. After my novel *Taps for Private Tussie* became a best seller in 1943, I was offered a lucrative position in Hollywood. But I decided that I would change worlds if I went there. I'd leave a world I knew, one that was my heritage and made me what I was, for a world that could quickly disinherit me if I didn't produce what I didn't know, where my heart and mind were not centered. I decided against going there. Had I gone to California to live, I wouldn't have settled in or near the largest cities, where I have spoken. I would have chosen Sacramento. Still, along the highway up the west coast of California, overlooking the Pacific, are some other choice places to live, to have a few acres around a home, and to see the sunsets over the Pacific.

Alaska is the only American state where I have not visited. I've been in Hawaii three times to speak. In my youth I read poems of this romantic land, and thrived on and loved the songs of Hawaii. I've been on all the islands except the small, unpopulated ones. I think Hawaii is a great place to visit, but it's not the place I would want to live. I'd choose, as I have, the continental United States.

But the United States is a fabulous land from the Atlantic to the Pacific and from the Gulf of Mexico to Canada. When one of my students at American University in Cairo asked me once why so many Americans didn't speak but one language, my reply was instant: "They don't have to speak but one language. Get in a car at Bar Harbor, Maine, and drive all the way across the North American continent to San Francisco, California, on the Pacific Coast, a distance of over 3,000 miles, and only the English language is spoken." This answer convinced my student.

Any state in America is a good place to live, any place you see the American flag, the stars and stripes forever flying. How many times in foreign countries I have gone to the American embassies to see our flag flying. When we travel for long hitches we get hungry to see our flag. I know I'm fortunate to live in America, and my selection of a place to live is just a matter of choosing.

MY WORLD

THERE ARE PLACES in this world where I have lived, worked, and visited, and where I would like to settle for a time. There are so many beautiful places I would have to be a thousand people to live for a time in each of them.

Two such places are in Scotland, land of my ancestors. I would like Inverness and a farm on the North Sea east of Edinburgh, a farm I'd like to own. In England, I'd choose Kent, somewhere in the southern part, where I could have a few acres and some apple trees and could see the English Channel. In France, I'd like a place on the Mediterranean near Marseille. In Italy, I'd choose the small town of Sorento, where leaves on the trees whisper about the well-known people from all over the world who have come here to live.

In Sweden, I'd choose Göteborg. In Norway, it would be Bergen, a beautiful northern city where I've been many times. In Finland, I'd choose Helsinki. I've never forgotten the old city of Tallinn, Estonia, which I knew before it became a part of Russia. In Iran, certainly it would be "the poets' city," Shiraz. What a clean and wonderful city! In Pakistan, it would have to be Rudyard Kipling's old city, Lahore.

In Burma, I'd choose Rangoon, one of the really pretty cities on earth, close to the Bay of Bengal, which is, I believe, the most beautiful bay in the world. In Thailand I'd take Bangkok. In the Philippines I'd choose Dumaguete or Cebu. I've worked in many parts of this country. I could live a full year in the Philippines, a tropical world of rain forests, land of forty-two species of lizards, of big snakes. In Taiwan, a friendly progressive country, I'd choose T'aipei first and T'aichung second.

South of the American border, I'll take somewhere on the Yucatán Peninsula of Mexico, or Guatemala City, certainly an attractive, ancient city with everything an American would want in a picturesque, high, and beautiful land. In Canada, I'd take Nova Scotia or Prince Edward Island.

When I travel I know I'm not a regionalist. I'm a world citizen. The world belongs to me. I can never get enough of life, of living, breathing the fresh winds in Kentucky, America, the world. But there are three countries, Greece, Egypt, and Lebanon, where my wife Naomi has visited seventeen times and I have visited sixteen. I'd like to live for a time in each of these countries.

One of my favorite places in the world to live for a while would be in the small yet large country of Lebanon. Not only do the seasons invite me, but the beauty and topography of this ancient land as well, land of the Phoenicians, Greeks, Romans, and now Christians and Moslems. Here men excavate down deep and find Phoenician antiques; less deep they find Greek vases and glasses; and still less deep are Roman artifacts. Here Christ and his disciples once walked, talked, and preached.

The Lebanese people fascinate me. They are the friendliest and most hospitable people of any I've visited in the world. They have distinctive food and believe me they eat well. They have strong family ties. Through my wife's people, the Norrises, we have relatives, the Zachems, in Lebanon.

Now where would I choose to live in Lebanon? I would choose first Beirut, one of the most attractive cities in the world. Here I would have a home or an apartment with windows and doors facing the Mediterranean Sea. The windows and doors of all homes face the Mediterranean in this ancient, beautiful city. And I would look from my window to see a sunset over the Mediterranean. At least once a week I would eat a meal of onion soup at the Phoenician Hotel, as I have done many times. There are stores in Beirut with everything you can get in America. The Lebanese are like their ancestors, the Phoenicians, the greatest traders on earth. Beirut could be called the city of beauty, of sunsets, sunrises, sparkling Mediterranean waters, without wastes along its streets or highways, a city where I could live in peace and contentment.

Also if I lived there I might possibly teach at American University of Beirut (AUB), recognized as America's greatest school outside of the United States. When I lectured there in 1962, students at AUB spoke fifty-eight different languages.

Lebanon has 4,105 square miles, approximately twelve times the size of my Greenup County, with its 350 square miles and a population of 35,000, or about 100 people to the square mile. Lebanon has between three and four million people, more than Kentucky, which is ten times as large in area.

If I lived in Lebanon I couldn't buy much land. I own a thousand acres in W-Hollow. I couldn't own one acre in the city limits of Beirut. When I priced that land in 1962 it sold by the square foot, the square yard. I figured the price of an acre in American dollars of 1962 value: eight million dollars plus, higher than in New York City. Who would buy it? An Arab investor would buy an acre (not too many left) and build a home. What are eight million dollars to men who drive gold Cadillacs? I priced other acres in Lebanon. Even the rocky slopes of goat pasture sold for $2,500 an acre. So I would probably compromise with an apartment in Beirut.

In the big small country of Lebanon I could live, if not in Beirut, then in ancient Byblos or Tyre or Tripoli, and drive daily up and down the Mediterranean coast. Or I could live in Zahle, over across a low mountain from Beirut in the Becca Valley, the "bread basket" of Lebanon, an area mentioned in the Bible, where the Romans raised grain to feed their cavalry horses. In this area was supposed to be the Tower of Babel. Here, too, American University of Beirut has its college of agriculture. Small, almost finger-size bananas and oranges grow here, as well as apples, pears, peaches, apricots, olives, and berries.

Lebanon is a country that has everything. I could live in Lebanon and be happy. I could drive over a mountain into the fertile Becca Valley, or across it and over a second mountain into Syria, and on to Damascus or north to Aleppo, as my wife and I once traveled. Or, I could drive up and down the coastal highway from Beirut to Tripoli, watching sunrises and sunsets forever. And the amazing thing is, I believe Lebanon is one of the few countries outside America where I could make a living by writing.

Another place I'd like to live is Egypt, where Naomi, our daughter Jane, and I spent one year, in 1960–1961. Naomi taught second grade at the private American School in El Ma'adi, a suburb of Cairo, and I taught English and education at American University in Cairo, while Jane took her freshman year at AUC.

We have been all over Egypt, but the one place I'd want to live is where we did live, in Zamalek on the Island of Gezeriah, surrounded by the Nile. I'd want to live on the side of the island facing the Nile Hilton Hotel. We lived on the second story of a seven-story stone house where we could stand on our balcony and throw an apple core into the Nile near the bulrushes where it was said Pharaoh's daughter found Moses. We watched busloads of world tourists pass our door and stop and get out on the tree-lined street near the bulrushes. Hundreds, maybe thousands, came to Gezeriah Island, the most scenic part of Cairo, the most attractive city in all Egypt and perhaps one of the most beautiful areas in the world that I have seen.

The idea of returning to Egypt to live for a short time fascinates me. It brings back old memories. Since we lived in Egypt we have returned six times, our last visit in the summer of 1972. Each time we return we take a taxi, cross the Nile by Tehira Bridge, and drive down the tree-shaded lane in Zamalek to the place where we once lived. We traveled this way many times in a Morris Minor driven by Dr. Carl Leiden, who also taught at AUC. The Carl Leidens and the Jesse Stuarts were the only American families on this heavily populated island surrounded by the Nile and the city of Cairo, a city grown to four millions.

Egypt is perhaps the oldest country in the world. An object isn't an antique there unless it's a thousand years old. Everywhere the ancient gods look up or down. A short distance from where we lived stood three pyramids and the Sphinx. We learned by living in Egypt that our America was a young, fresh country.

The Nile Valley that grew our food had black topsoil ninety-two feet deep, the deepest topsoil in the world. The farmers along the Nile have worked this soil for five thousand years. Five thousand years ago they were ninety-two feet below where they work the soil now. We saw men, women, and children working in the fields together. Once I went down to a field and plowed with a yoke of white heifers, broke the fertile Nile soil with a sharp-pointed plow to show the Egyptian farmers that an American schoolteacher could plow with cattle. They were so pleased they offered me coffee they had made in a pot over a fire. Their fuel was dried sheep dung. There is no rain, only sun along the Nile. Everything is dry. Bodies buried in the sand on the west bank of the Nile, the sunset side, never decay. On the east bank, where the sun rises, there is life and bodies aren't buried.

The Egyptians are beautiful people, friendly people. Once they had the greatest civilization in the world. They made pyramids that couldn't be made today. They made steel that would bend double. The embalmed bodies lying in state in the National Museum have lasted 3,500 years. The ancient Egyptians had secrets that have been lost to the world.

We didn't own a car in Egypt. We went places with the Leidens, both families, seven people, in their little Morris Minor, a car we never owned but shared and will never forget. And we went places by taxi. Going by taxi was reasonable. Everything was reasonable compared to prices in the United States and Europe. There wasn't any food in cans. We had fresh vegetables and fruits from the gardens and trees. Each of the twelve months brought different fruits and vegetables. And we had the best steaks there we'd ever eaten anywhere.

I couldn't buy shirts or pajamas ready made in stores in Egypt, but I had them made. Each time I return to Egypt now I have pajamas made, best in the world, out of their long-staple cotton.

Life was easy in Egypt compared to life in America. We had a man who cooked for us, purchased our food, and kept our apartment clean, a large Nubian whose name was Salah Ramadian. Had we continued to live in Egypt, we would have kept Salah as long as he lived. The Stuart family became attached to him. This was the way of life in Egypt.

One evening in the summer of 1972, while we were staying at the Nile Hilton Hotel, Naomi and I sat on our balcony watching the boats on the Nile. The feluccas were going upstream, for this is the way the wind blows constantly. Their sails were spread and full of wind. Other boats came down with the current. Transportation on the Nile, the wind taking the boats up and the current bringing them down, hadn't cost anything as long as there had been an Egypt.

I told Naomi that I'd like to return to Egypt and teach again at AUC. I had never taught youth as bright, youth who had more respect for education, school properties, and their teachers. Of course, not all the students enrolled at AUC came from Egypt. Some came from Arab countries in Africa and the Middle East, from Europe, and some from the United States. They came from all over the world.

"But time is fleeting for us," Naomi reminded me. "We don't have enough time left to live all the places you'd like to live. I doubt we will ever live here again. But we can return for visits."

All around us were the lights of Cairo. The lights loomed up and made a bright canopy in the sky. Higher up there was another canopy of starlight. Down below us flowed the mighty Nile, the most famous river in the world, loaded with traffic that would be moving all night and all day tomorrow. I'd like to live in Cairo again, beside the Nile in Zamalek on the Island of Gezeriah, and teach at American University in Cairo.

If I were to choose a country to live in out of all the European countries, I would not choose Scotland, or England, or Ireland, as wonderful and beautiful as they are. I would choose Greece. In my youth I cannot remember ever having seen a Greek. As great as their culture has been to the world, I knew very little about it. I didn't have any special interest in Greek culture.

But in the spring of 1937 I went to Scotland on a Guggenheim Fellowship and took a room near the University of Edinburgh for fourteen months. From there I traveled through the British Isles, Ireland, the Scandinavian countries, and the mainland of Europe. On my way home I visited the Balkan countries and took the Orient Express down the Danube, through northern Greece, and into Turkey, my twenty-sixth country. My plan was to visit Turkey, then sail on a small Italian ship from Istanbul through the Aegean Sea and the Corinth Canal to the Ionian Sea and on to Genoa, Italy, where I would sail home on the Countess Savoy. But meeting two young English teachers from England who taught at

Roberts College, Istanbul, changed all of this. When we reached Piraeus, we got off the ship and walked up to Athens, a distance of eight miles, carrying our suitcases. This was one of the fine decisions of my life.

These two Englishmen were going to Greece to take unto themselves Greek brides. I asked them why Greek brides when there were so many women in England, Wales, Scotland, and Ireland, and not enough men for them. "Wait until you see the beautiful Greek women," said one. "Wait until you stay in Greece! How long will it be?"

"Until the Countess Savoy sails from Genoa to New York and returns," I said. "I have a ticket to return on the Countess Savoy."

I parted with the young teachers and went to King George I Hotel, where a room cost $2.50 a day, with a reduction if I stayed a week or more. Money was now a factor with me. I'd been living away from home, traveling second and third class. I had lived a student's life in Edinburgh, not wasting a dollar. I'd sold stories for small fees to English magazines to supplement my $2,000 fellowship. These were strong, great American dollars in 1938.

In Greece I discovered that what the Englishmen had told me was true. I liked the Greek food and music. I believe I saw everything in Athens and visited the Parthenon several times. I also visited Corinth, Thermopylae, Samales, Thebes. I bought recordings and English translations of Greek books. I'd found a land and a people whose heroism and creativity in all fields of endeavor fascinated me. Here I found the bluest sky and prettiest sunsets I had ever seen. And there was scarcely any area where I could not hear the sound of the sea. The winds blew everywhere. The winds blew strong. I knew I'd return to this country, and I have many times since 1938, with Naomi and our daughter Jane, who went to school in Athens and speaks Greek. We lived in Athens and I spoke in many places in Greece for the United States Information Service.

Now, of all the ninety countries in the world where I have visited (and Naomi has visited most of these), our preference for one to live in would be Greece. There are excellent places to live all over the mainland, down in the Peloponnesus, or on the many islands in the Mediterranean. There are more than a hundred suitable areas to live in. But there is one I'd choose above all others. What a place it would be to spend six months or a year. Many Greeks who have made their money in America have returned to this area, built fine homes, and retired here. I cannot blame them for this. They have chosen wisely.

This scenic spot of earth is the ancient state of Attica, with Athens as its capital. The southernmost part of Attica is Cape Sounion, and here on the southernmost tip is the Temple of Poseidon, god of the sea, that Greek sailors look forward to seeing on their return from foreign lands. Here, too, are olive orchards, grape vines, wheat fields, and pastures for sheep, goats, and donkeys. Here are villages with narrow, rainbow streets and old houses—I don't know how old—one-story with moss-covered tile roofs. But there are also large, beautiful, American-style houses. No wonder Greeks from foreign countries have returned here. English and American and some German families live here, too.

I would like to own or rent one of the American-style houses, just the size for Naomi and me and the guests we might have, with modern conveniences, running water, heat, air conditioning, and a plot of ground, perhaps an acre, with a grape arbor, olive, peach, apple, and lemon trees and a garden. And I would want to live where I could look upon the waters of the Aegean Sea. Our home could be anywhere from Porta Rafti on the east coast down to Cape Sounion, the thumb of old Attica jutting out into the Aegean. On the west coast of this thumb we could live happily anywhere from Vorkiza down Via Anavessos to Surieon. A road connects these three coastal villages. On this west side of Attica we would look from our home upon the waters of the Saronic Gulf, which separates Attica from the Peloponnesus. We'd see the Saronic waters meet the Aegean Sea. Blue waters, blue air, and blue sky! And here the winds blow constantly. I call this area Sounion the Beautiful. I've written a published article on this area.

And I would like to have a small Italian or German car. A fine road runs around the southernmost tip of Attica, with just room for two cars to pass. There is a little Greek restaurant here, just under the bank and above the Aegean Sea. Naomi and I found this restaurant when we first visited Greece together. It's been there a long time. We ate octopus tentacles and seaweed soup here. It was so good we've been back every time we've been to Greece. Both of us like seafood. If we lived in this area we'd be here often. We'd bring our guests here, for this would be a treat for them.

Attica, which produced the world's most learned men, would be my choice spot to live outside my native Kentucky and the United States. I would take Attica over Sparta, which produced the world's greatest soldiers. I would take Attica over Macedonia, Thessaly, Thrace, or the Peloponnesus.

On the southern tip of old Attica I could have fruit, grapes, olives. I could grow a garden. All of this would be fun. No wonder so many people from Western countries, young people and old, live on the Greek mainland and on the islands. What a beautiful, clean country! Nothing thrown on the streets or along the highways. An ancient country with one of the greatest civilized people who ever walked on the face of the earth. The Egyptians educated for death. The Greeks educated for life.

Southern Attica would be the ideal location. Roads lead from here all over Greece. Naomi and I would want to travel. Also, we'd be only an hour from the Athens airport or from the seaport of Piraeus. To take small trips by boats to all the coastal villages, to have boat and ship service as the ancient Greeks did would be one of the greatest joys in our lives. Here under the blue sky, in the sun and wind, with the sound of waters lapping along the rocky shores, would be the ideal place to spend part of the last years we have to live.

Then there is another reason for selecting this area of Greece for a temporary home. Each time I drove over roads going toward the Temple of Poseidon, I would know that many of the ancient Greeks, even those who lived in Athens before the temple was built, and certainly after it was built, came this way. They walked the forty-three miles from Athens to Landsend or Sounion, or they rode donkeys and came in carts. They came down from Athens by sailboat along the coast of the Saronic Gulf. These Greeks loved their native land. They loved Athens and Attica, and left their mark on its culture with their literature, architecture, art, and philosophy. So, on roads where I'd drive or on soil where I'd step I'd wonder how many of the great Greeks had stepped here hundreds and thousands of years ago.

But there would be a flaw in my living here all the year. I couldn't live here in autumn. I'd have to return to my W-Hollow, my Greenup County, to see the multicolored leaves on the trees. I'd have to be out in a strong October or early November wind that would sweep millions of leaves from the trees upward toward a blue autumn sky, up and down to earth again. I don't have too many autumns left perhaps, and I want to make each one count to my fullest appreciation and enjoyment, for Kentucky autumns are seasons of physical poetry.

Autumn in Greece, like all other seasons of the year, is green. The cypress, pine, and olive trees are silver in spring, summer, and autumn. I haven't found red autumn leaves in Greece, not leaves as red as sourwood, sassafras, black sumac, red sumac, black gum, sweet gum, and maple. There isn't another autumn in the world like the one in my native land. Greece in all seasons has a serious mood. The winds blow perpetually over the rugged lands, the gulfs and seas. Water surges constantly against the rocky banks. There is a serious sadness in these roars, as if the voices of the long departed are disturbed about what is happening to the land they loved and knew.

In a Kentucky autumn, among the billions of bright leaves, there is laughter in the wind. There is joy. Wind and leaves make poetry together. And this is the place I have to be. I've said I'll never miss another Kentucky autumn, and I won't. But the rest of my year would be spent in Greece, my chosen country in the world, this great historical and sacred land.

Here is my world, then, from W-Hollow to Attica in Greece. I own the deed to some of the acres in my W-Hollow. I own other land in Kentucky, across the United States and around the world through my travels and my memories. Wherever I have visited, spoken, lived, I have tried to bring to that place what my father brought to W-Hollow: eyes to find and see, a mind to know, and a heart to appreciate. And through my writing, through this book, I have tried to share the beauty, the wonder, the hardships, and the joys of this world I have known: my world, your world, our world.